Hidden Holiness

Hidden Holiness

Unwrapping the Gift of God's Presence

BY DAVID M. CRUMP
Foreword by John D. Witvliet

CASCADE *Books* · Eugene, Oregon

HIDDEN HOLINESS
Unwrapping the Gift of God's Presence

Copyright © 2025 David M. Crump. All rights reserved. Except for brief quotations in critical publications or reviews, no part of this book may be reproduced in any manner without prior written permission from the publisher. Write: Permissions, Wipf and Stock Publishers, 199 W. 8th Ave., Suite 3, Eugene, OR 97401.

Cascade Books
An Imprint of Wipf and Stock Publishers
199 W. 8th Ave., Suite 3
Eugene, OR 97401

www.wipfandstock.com

PAPERBACK ISBN: 979-8-3852-0488-5
HARDCOVER ISBN: 979-8-3852-0489-2
EBOOK ISBN: 979-8-3852-0490-8

Cataloguing-in-Publication data:

Names: Crump, David M., author. | Witvliet, John D., foreword.

Title: Hidden holiness : unwrapping the gift of God's presence / David M. Crump; foreword by John D. Witvliet.

Description: Eugene, OR: Cascade Books, 2025 | Includes bibliographical references.

Identifiers: ISBN 979-8-3852-0488-5 (paperback) | ISBN 979-8-3852-0489-2 (hardcover) | ISBN 979-8-3852-0490-8 (ebook)

Subjects: LCSH: Holiness—Christianity. | Holiness—Biblical teaching. | Sanctification—Biblical teaching.

Classification: BT767 C815 2025 (paperback) | BT767 (ebook)

VERSION NUMBER 05/19/25

Contents

Foreword by John D. Witvliet | vii
Acknowledgments | xiii
Introduction: Holy Cow! Holy God? | xv

Chapter One
Hallowed Be Thy Name | 1

Chapter Two
The Holy, Wholly Other One | 12

Chapter Three
Seeing the Invisible, Knowing the Unknowable God | 24

Chapter Four
The Problem with "the Problem" of Divine Violence | 36

Chapter Five
Holiness Becomes Relational | 49

Chapter Six:
Be Holy as I Am Holy | 63

Chapter Seven
Holiness Is Proven by Its Justice | 77

Chapter Eight
Holiness, History and the End of It All | 91

Bibliography | 105
Scripture Index | 109
Subject Index | 115

Foreword

THE WORD "HOLY" IS among the most frequently used words in the history of Christian worship. In ancient and still-used Eastern Orthodox liturgies, the prayer "Holy God, Holy Mighty, Holy Immortal, have mercy on us" is an oft-repeated prayer. In ancient Western liturgies that are adapted for contemporary weekly use in Roman Catholic, Anglican, Episcopalian, and many Methodist, Lutheran, and Presbyterian churches, the acclamation "Holy, holy, holy Lord, God of power and might, heaven and earth are full of your glory" is sung or spoken in a prominent place in the eucharistic prayer. One of the most commonly shared ecumenical English language hymns is "Holy, holy, holy! Lord God Almighty! Early in the morning our song shall rise to Thee; Holy, holy, holy! merciful and mighty! God in three Persons, blessed Trinity!" Among the most frequently sung contemporary evangelical and Pentecostal worship songs are those with titles such as "Holy Forever," "Holy Ground," and "Only a Holy God." In each of these very different contexts, some of Christianity's most poignant, compelling, and memorable music has been reserved for setting these acclamations of holiness—from ancient plainchant melodies to grand choral settings of the Sanctus in masses by Palestrina, Bach, and Mozart, from exuberant congregational choruses sung in Kenya, Indonesia, Korea, and Pakistan to newly written chants for use in cathedrals in Norway, Italy, Brazil and India. For twenty centuries, in two hundred-plus countries, and in a vast number of denominations,

Foreword

over two billion Christian believers have been invited to acclaim God as the Holy One.

That frequency of use, however, does not mean that the term is well understood or appreciated. For the past several years, I have taught courses on theology and Christian worship and learned a great deal from my students about their perceptive judgement that the term "holiness" may be one of the most misunderstood terms in regular Christian usage. They have helped me clarify at least three challenges related to how the term is often understood—even when, or especially when, that definition is never explicitly articulated.

One challenge is that while the term is usually thought of as referring to something good, it is not always associated with something beautiful, compelling, or deeply desirable. If someone told these students "have a holy weekend," they might not perceive it as very warm and joyful invitation. "Holiness" has often become associated with being "holier than thou," with being judgmental, legalistic, dull, and boring. Then it doesn't seem to have much to do with the quintessential convergence of that which is good, true, beautiful, that which fulfills our deepest, unspoken desires. Christianity has a long history of distinguishing how to be spirituality judicious without being judgmental, to love God's law without being legalistic, to cherish the wonders of creation in ways that resist the drab and dull. Practicing these distinctions by using this book will help us polish up our working definition of holiness.

A second recurring challenge emerges when we routinely sing "holy, holy, holy" about and to God, but fail to see holiness as a good, right, true, beautiful part of our calling as believers—and an integral part of the salvation offered to us in Jesus and effected by the Holy Spirit. We slip into a view of Christianity that highlights justification (the stunning gift of God's) but minimizes sanctification. I routinely hear from students who grew up in churches that regularly celebrate the divine action of justification and routinely rehearse scriptural commands that guide our obedience. They repeatedly confirm their impression that God is at work in the first arena, but the second arena is left up to us. They have missed

Foreword

anything resembling the Christian doctrine of sanctification: the vision of how God is at work not only forgiving sin but also making each us and all of us collectively in Christ into saints—God's holy people. This book will help correct this imbalance, inviting us to contemplate not only scriptural depictions of divine holiness, but also the graces that attend to noticing how God's Spirit helps believers to respond to scripture's call to "Be holy as I am holy," to become God's "holy priesthood."

A third definitional challenge my students have noticed is the way in which functional definitions of holiness have become otherworldly in ways that scriptural treatments of the term are not. To be sure, Scripture speaks of holiness in terms of separation from all that is unholy. Holiness involves purification from all that is worldly. At the same time, Scripture also presents robust connections between holiness and embodied practices of justice. Separation from the "world" in this sense is in no way a separation from embodied practices. My students will appreciate the care that Dr. Crump has taken to pay deep attention to this challenge. These same students would wisely protest if some future professor would assign chapter 2 of this book without chapter 7 (or vice versa). Indeed, as Dr. Crump suggests, each chapter of this book attends to an essential element of a scriptural vision of holiness. The most robustly biblical treatment of holiness will insist that the term must embrace both prophetic and priestly themes, that it is entirely bound up in both righteousness and justice, terms that may be used differently but which at the best are intimately intertwined.

In sum, we need to work on how we understand this term. And while it is true that our working understanding of *every* Bible and theological term is in need of repair and refinement, attention to this central and important terms seems especially urgent.

Importantly, in these classroom discussions I have noticed that the moments of new insight and learning (for me as much as for my students) have come not primarily from confronting underdeveloped or off-base understandings of holiness (via negative) but rather from dwelling with the positive, compelling, and altogether astonishing aspects of how the Bible treats holiness (via positive). It's important not just to say what holiness isn't, but also what it is—what it looks like. How remarkable it is that God commanded Israel to establish a small beachhead of holiness within time and space by constructing a temple—a temple with the "holy of holies" at its center. What wonder there is in Ezekiel's vision of streams of holiness and shalom that flow out from the temple with such hyperbolic surplus that its outflow crescendoes over time (Ezek 47). How remarkable it is that true holiness became incarnate within time and space. How remarkable it is that we are called to be saints, God's holy priesthood—living in time and space as beachheads of holiness in our congregations, neighborhoods, and workplaces. Holiness emerges in space and time, and its aroma is the aroma of Jesus. Here, too, this book blesses us with positive visions of a Christocentric vision, a vision of divine holiness accommodated to human capacity.

For all these reasons, I am deeply grateful for this theological exploration of holiness. I warmly encourage you, as Dr. Crump suggests, to read this book slowly with your Bible readily available. If you begin to highlight every passage he discusses here and then to notice these texts in their context, you will see afresh the beautiful ways the entire Bible coheres. For those who wish to engage further, I would also warmly encourage reading David Crump's other published works to notice the echoes and resonances of material presented here. His writings on prayer (*Knocking on Heaven's Door*), citizenship (*I Pledge Allegiance*), and conflict in the Middle East (*Like Birds in a Cage: Christian Zionism's Collusion in Israel's Oppression of the Palestinian People*) not only correspond with themes discussed here, but also show the larger implications of holiness for how we express love of both God and neighbor.

Still further, let me make one more suggestion from the worship and theology course classroom I love to spend time in. Consider developing your own "holiness musical playlist" of profoundly weighty and compelling music that focuses on this seminal divine attribute. Words alone can refine our working understanding of a term. Music is such a profound gift for helping our hearts and wills catch up with our minds. Listen to the Sanctus of J. S. Bach's B Minor Mass or Faure's Requiem or Boniface Mganga's Missa Luba. Notice how many styles of music can be drawn up to bring the hymns "Holy, Holy, Holy" or "Take Time to Be Holy" to life. I am always grateful when students curate their own playlists of worship-related songs. Together we discover that many different styles and approaches to music can contribute a lot to our own devotional, worshipful engagement with God. Together we discover that songs about holiness can be weighty and still entirely accessible, full of grandeur and wonder while also being surprisingly exuberant or while contemplative. When our analysis of all this begins to run dry of new insights or tires from mental fatigue, we marvel at how God's Spirit can surprise us by coaxing us into moments when our speech about God gives way to speech that addresses God, and we find ourselves "lost in wonder, love, and praise." May all readers of this book be graced in that way.

> Dr. John D. Witvliet
> Calvin Institute of Christian Worship

Acknowledgments

I MUST BEGIN BY thanking my editors Michael Thomson and George Callihan. Their diligent attention to the content, style, and formatting of my manuscript have made this a better book than it would otherwise have been. Though, if the reader still does not like the book's content, the responsibility falls solely on my shoulders. Perhaps one day we can discuss our disagreements about what it means for God to be a holy God and the resulting contours of holiness in the Christian life.

I also need to thank friends who offered important feedback on earlier versions of this book. Thank you, Marla and Gene, for commenting on the first draft of an incomplete manuscript in the early days of this project. Special thanks to Rick, a staff member at my local church, who went through the manuscript's penultimate version with a fine-tooth comb. Our lengthy coffee drinking session at a local deli was especially helpful.

As always, I must give special thanks to my wife, Terry, who is always my first reader and most important critic.

Introduction
Holy Cow! Holy God?

BLASPHEMY COMES IN ALL shapes and sizes.[1] At least from the perspective of the blasphemer abusing the name of God and God's character can occur on a sliding scale from mild to wild, depending on the social circles in which a person feels most comfortable. Many of the most loquacious blasphemers will not recognize this category of speech at all, seeing no difference between an exclamatory "holy cow!" and the expletive "holy @#*!" Though neither expression has any relation to the idea of divine holiness, peppering our angry, shocked, disgruntled outbursts of disapproval with out-of-place God language is a deeply embedded human tendency. Invoking God or God's attributes adds hefty emphasis to whatever we want to say. Even the ancient Greeks were as prone to say, "Oh my god" or "by Zeus!"[2] just as many modern Americans exclaim, "Oh my God!" without giving an inkling of thought to what they have just said. God's name and attributes become a handy exclamation mark, the verbal equivalent of boldface on the printed page.

Blasphemy often becomes so normalized that entire societies employ it openly, deliberately, without hesitation.

---

1. Blasphemy means being disrespectful towards the things of God.
2. The ancient Greeks could refer either to "god" or to "Zeus," with the same effect; for a few examples see Aristophanes, *Birds*, 15. Pisthetearus, answering a question about the direction of a journey indicated by a crow says, "By Zeus, it no longer croaks the same thing it did."

Introduction

Declaring Human Affairs Holy

Blasphemy has to do with making inappropriate, flippant, or casual use of things that are divine or holy. But what is holiness? Our culture is quite confused about what makes something holy. Presidents, senators, clergy, and other community leaders regularly bow their heads at the base of what used to be the Twin Towers in New York City and all agree that they are standing on "holy ground." But what makes that piece of real estate holy? What does that mean, precisely? Many Americans (and others) died there as the innocent victims of al-Qaida terrorists. This proved to be a catalyst for America's war against "terror." But the question arises, does human bloodshed sanctify a plot of ground? If these events made America's war a holy war, then what is it that makes war, of all things, holy? In the Old Testament, when the God of Israel, Yahweh, went to battle against Israel's enemies, that may be understood as a type of holy war. But nowadays, who can determine which side God is on? Indeed, is God on anybody's side? Perhaps the Creator of all things is standing on the sidelines shaking his head at the gross arrogance and stupidity of human pretensions.

Certainly, one of the most remarkable examples of senseless "holy war" was World War I, a war in which millions upon millions of men, women, and children died for who knows what reason. At least, that was the verdict of Harry Patch, the last combat veteran of the "Great War" to die at age 111 in 2009. As retold in Philip Jenkins's book, *The Great and Holy War: How World War I Became a Religious Crusade*, that war was a senseless waste of human lives with no particular meaning or purpose, as European nations butchered each other for their own narrow, nationalist purposes. "What the hell we fought for I now don't know," said Mr. Patch shortly before he died.[3] What the hell, indeed. The religious fervor associated with this carnage was blasphemous to the core, in that it blithely attributed to God matters, not of frivolity this time, but of horror that had no basis in the God of Scripture.

---

3. Jenkins, *Great and Holy War*, 3.

Introduction

The blasphemous irony of so-called holy war is that all parties insist they and they alone are God's army fighting for the cause of righteousness. In World War I, England, France, Germany, and the United States each claimed that it alone was the singularly Christian nation called by divine providence to crush the demonic enemy. Calling the war "holy" justified every extreme, sanctifying the most profane actions imaginable. For instance, an especially fervent Methodist church leader, George W. Downs, freely included his own ghoulish wartime fantasies in his Sunday sermons, confessing to parishioners that he wished he could charge the trenches with other soldiers where, he said, "I would drive my bayonet into the throat or the eye or the stomach of the Huns without the slightest hesitation."[4]

Just as frivolous or disrespectful references to God can be used as casual exclamation marks, so also the language of holiness or sanctification can be used to grant the appearance of divine approval for the most heinous human actions. The problem, of course, is that this way of thinking inverts the influence towards the holy, understanding the way holiness is imparted completely the wrong way around. Can human beings make something holy simply by calling it holy? Or, does authentic holiness proceed from God to sanctify a person, place, or thing as God determines? Who gets to apply divine holiness?

Answering such questions from the point of view of the Christian faith requires that we have a proper understanding of holiness to begin with. How does Scripture define holiness? What does it mean for God to be a holy God? What are we saying when people or places are described as holy? And what does personal holiness mean for the way Christians ought to live their lives?

What Lies Ahead

This book's structure first took shape years ago, arising from a biblical survey course I taught at Calvin University. Some years later,

---

4. Cited in Jenkins, *Great and Holy War*, 94.

Introduction

I find myself working out these original ideas here for you, my readers.

The book is divided into three sections. Section one is composed of four chapters that examine the meaning of attributing holiness to God. When Scripture conveys the words of the Lord saying: "Be holy because I am holy" (Lev 11:44–45; 1 Pet 1:16), what are we being told about the nature and personality of God? What does it mean for our God to be a holy God?

Section two, chapter five, expands the definition of holiness beyond what it means for God to be holy in and of himself. Here we come to terms with the relational nature of divine holiness. As God says "Be holy because I am holy," Scripture testifies to a personal relationship between the Holy One and the recipient of God's revelation. What, then, does the relational dimension of holiness look like? What does it mean for sinners, such as you and I, to live in personal relationship with a holy God?

Section three, composed of chapters six through eight, explores the ethical dimension of holiness. God's holiness command requires a moral response. The command, "Be holy because I am holy" proffers a new way of living, a new holy lifestyle that is in contrast to an old, profane lifestyle. God's word is a call to transformation. What does that transformation look like? What thoughts and behaviors characterize a holy life? In what ways is the believer's holy life related to God's own holy life?

Of course, a great deal more could be said in answer to such questions than is contained in this book. It is my hope that every reader who picks up *Hidden Holiness* will finish the book from beginning to end. I have been succinct to encourage that response. Each section is equally important as the next. Shorter chapters were crafted to encourage the reader to finish a given chapter in a single sitting.

Second, my hope is that this book will be read slowly, thoughtfully, prayerfully, and meditatively. Ideally, the reader will keep a Bible close at hand. There are many Scripture references that are vital to consider for a proper understanding of holiness to be truly scriptural and Christian. I encourage the reader to take the time to look up the references and to read them. Take time to consider the wider context of these passages. Pray and contemplate the meaning of the text and its personal significance. Carefully weigh and consider the exposition provided in this book as your mind and heart progress through each chapter.

A brief word about my approach here is worthwhile. I approach the Scriptures from a strictly canonical point of view. That is, I assume that the same divine mind is behind all the books of the Old and New Testaments so that they all speak with one voice. Aside from the obvious differences between the old and the new covenants embodied in the Old and New Testament, I do not seek to trace out the individual voices or perspectives of the different biblical writers. For instance, when working in the Old Testament I will refer to texts from the law, the prophets, and the writings with one breath, without distinction.[5] For my purposes here, it's all the word of God given to us and for us.

One of my seminary professors was J. I. Packer, who used to say that all theology is doxology, giving glory to God. My hope and my prayer are that *Hidden Holiness* will not only teach the reader *about* God's holiness, but that it may also facilitate the *experience* of God's holiness as head knowledge and heart knowledge become one. Ideally, this process of learning theology as doxology will result in more and more brothers and sisters in Christ offering more and more praise and adoration to the Holy One and his one and only Son, the resurrected Savior, Jesus Christ our Lord.

For God alone deserves all our praise.

Soli Deo Gloria

---

5. For those interested in learning more about the individual Old Testament witnesses to holiness, I recommend John G. Gammie's *Holiness in Israel*.

Chapter One

Hallowed Be Thy Name

JESUS SAT DOWN NEAR the crest of the hill as a crowd of followers gathered around. Many had been following him for some time. Others had only recently heard the news about the man from Nazareth who worked miracles and announced the imminent arrival of God's kingdom come to earth.

The twelve disciples—men that Jesus called his apostles, his messengers, because they also traveled the countryside replicating Jesus' ministry of teaching, healing the sick, and casting evil spirits out of the oppressed—sat on the grass next to Jesus as the gathering crowd swelled in numbers. The hillside became a small open-air theater beneath blue sky and billowing clouds, with the traveling Galilean taking center stage. Soon newcomers were forced to stand if they hoped to catch a glimpse of Jesus through the waves of shifting heads and bobbing shoulders straining to follow his every word.

As Jesus formed this new community, this new movement around himself, animated by a distinctive vision of life, several of his disciples had begun to wonder if Jesus' teaching about the kingdom of God had implications for their own personal piety. For instance, some questioned if they should alter their customary forms of prayer. How should they pray now as Jews who believe that Jesus is the messiah? Several disciples openly asked Jesus,

"Lord, what difference should your new teaching make to the way we pray?"

On this day, as the sun shone brightly and a gentle breeze rustled the grass, Jesus answered their question, "This is how you should pray: Father, hallowed be your name" (Matt 6:9–34; Luke 11:2–4 KJV).[1]

What Does It Mean to Hallow Something?

Hallowed is an old-fashioned English word that has gone out of style. It means "to make holy, sacred, consecrated." In newer translations, we are more likely to read something like, "Father, honor your name," (Good News Translation), "keep your name holy," (New International Standard Version), or "sanctify your name" (Tree of Life Version). But the meaning of Jesus' words is still far from obvious. What is he telling us to pray for? This first request, typically referred to as a petition, obviously has something to do with the holiness of God's name, but it is much more than a warning not to use God's name as a swear word.

In the Bible, God's name is often used as a stand-in for God himself, a way of designating God's holy person without explicitly mentioning God. For the writers of our Scriptures, talking about the eternal, all-powerful, holy Creator required both tremendous reverence and a measure of trepidation. It is important not to abuse the privilege of living in relationship with the Holy One, and a good way to safeguard that privilege was by using care and respect in the way people talked about God, whether in prayer or personal conversation. In the Old Testament, God is often referred to as Yahweh (Exod 3:13–15).[2] But rather than speak the holy name

---

1. For an extensive analysis of the Lord's Prayer, see my book *Knocking on Heaven's Door*, chapters 5, 6, and 7.

2. Without going into great detail, God's name is translated in Exodus 3:14–15 as "I am, I am who I am," or "I will be what I will be." In Exodus 3:12 the introduction of Yahweh's name is most closely associated with God's promise to always "be with" his people. Thus, God's name, Yahweh, becomes a divine promise of relational faithfulness. It is God's very nature to always be with his people.

Yahweh outright, many Old Testament writers offered greater reverence by speaking of "the Name," meaning God himself. Jewish readers and hearers of these texts were formed in that tradition such that they naturally understood to whom you were referring when using "the name" in this way.

So, when Jesus teaches the disciples to pray, "Father, cause your name to be holy," *he is teaching us to ask God to do something for himself*. Specifically, the disciples, and we who follow them in praying this way, are asking God to glorify himself, to unveil God's own sanctity, to reveal publicly the holiness of God's majestic personhood for all to see.

At several points in the biblical storyline, Yahweh's fearsome and awe-inspiring presence blows people away by simply showing up for an appointment. God does not need to be angry in order to have an overwhelming, intimidating effect on people. Yahweh only needs to put in an appearance.

When a shepherd named Moses investigated a curiously burning bush, he was quickly stopped in his tracks because his dirty sandals would mar God's "holy ground" (Exod 3:5–6). The story reveals that God's holiness is transferred to the things around him when he reveals himself, including the very soil that sustains the flaming shrubbery through which God revealed himself. God's holiness is automatically transferred to anything in contact with him, which is then either blessed (by also becoming holy) or destroyed (by being judged and condemned). The bush burns without being consumed but Moses hears a warning—or possibly a threat—to keep his distance.

When Yahweh "comes down" onto Mount Sinai in order to celebrate Israel's initiation into a new level of intimacy with their covenant-making, redeemer God, the entire congregation is warned to stand back. Yahweh's divine presence turned all of Mount Sinai into holy ground. It became the meeting place where God's people could come close to God's holy presence—but not too close. Excessive familiarity might cause the Holy One "to break out against them" even in this moment when he has promised to save them (Exod 19:22, 24).

When Moses later asked that he might "see God's glory," to have a more intimate encounter with the Holy One than was allowed at Mount Sinai, he was warned that "no one can see God and live" (Exod 33:20). Yet, acting upon the overflow of divine mercy (Exod 33:19), Yahweh responds by placing Moses into a man-sized crack in a nearby boulder. There, in his ready-made safety chamber, Moses discovered that viewing even the backside of God's glory was beyond his human comprehension (Exod 33:23). "Moses bowed to the ground at once and worshiped" (Exod 34:8). As descriptive language failed him, Moses was compelled to place his nose in the dirt and sing effusive, all-consuming adoration to the One who alone deserves all glory, praise, and honor (Exod 34:6–8).

Holy Unapproachability

The Scriptures reveal a long and rather strange history of God glorifying his name by revealing his threatening and unspeakable holiness to those seeking him. It seems that God can choose to approach us, but he then warns us not to approach him, at least not too closely, not without holy fear. It would seem that only God knows the proper distance needed between creature and Creator, the necessary space that is appropriate to both intimacy and reverent fear. God always remains in control of this dance. He knows and reveals what distance is a safe distance between we sinners and the Holy One. God can take the initiative of divine grace to approach us, but we are not therefore free to approach God under our own steam. We must follow God's instructions carefully. Those who do have such an encounter with God in the Scriptures speak of it in terms of both glory and fear.

The New Testament continues this theme of holy unapproachability as it tells the story of Jesus and reflects on the deep truths of his gospel message. Jesus is God coming to us. He is Emmanuel, God with us (Matt 1:23). Yet, the guidance Jesus provides for how sinners may approach God contains strict instructions, as will be explained in the chapters ahead.

Jesus teaches his disciples to pray to the same holy God who ages ago had warned Moses to take off his dirty shoes and to back away from holy ground. It shouldn't surprise us, then, to learn that Jesus, the new Moses who establishes a new covenant for a renewed people of God, also taught his followers to pray that their Holy Father would continue his pattern of self-revelation. So, Jesus taught his followers to say: Father, sanctify your name. Or, to put it another way:

Father, let the entire world feel the ineffable fury of your mercy; blind us by the brilliance of your strangeness; exalt yourself so that we are launched into the celestial fires of purification as you wrap your holy arms around us.

And do this, Father, not only for us, your people, but do it for the entire watching world. Display your infinite majesty incessantly to everyone, everywhere, until all of humanity bows down and confesses that "you alone are worthy, our Lord and God, to receive glory and honor and power" (Rev. 4:10).

Father, hallowed be your name.

Ezekiel's Vision of Hallowing the Name

I strongly suspect that Jesus had been meditating on the Old Testament prophet Ezekiel when he finally settled on the wording of this first petition.[3] Ezekiel prophesied to the Judean exiles who had been carried away by the Babylonian army into foreign captivity in 586 BC. They were enslaved by the Babylonians as Yahweh's punishment for their idolatrous covenant breaking. They had worshiped other gods and reveled in injustice. This wicked misbehavior, all performed while they bragged about being Yahweh's privileged, chosen people, had unleashed the judgment that God had warned them about generations earlier (Deut 28:15–68). That judgment meant exile and foreign captivity. So, Yahweh had stirred up the Babylonian empire calling them to give Israel a colossal, corrective heavenly spanking.

---

3. For additional discussion, see Crump, *Knocking on Heaven's Door*, 115–20.

Hidden Holiness

One of the results of Babylon's victory over Israel, perhaps the most important result as far as Yahweh was concerned, was the way in which the surrounding nations now slandered Israel's God for being a loser. Yahweh became the loser god of a loser people. His reputation was dragged through the mud since the Babylonian gods now appeared to have decisively trounced Yahweh on the battlefield, once and for all. He had been humiliated together with his defeated people. Or, as Ezekiel put it, Israel's misbehavior and punishment had "profaned God's name among the nations" (Ezek 36:20–23).[4]

Fortunately for Israel, however, Yahweh cares deeply about his public reputation. God not only remembered the covenant's warnings against disobedience but also the many promises about his never-ending covenant faithfulness. Yahweh will not abandon the chosen people forever. They *will* be rescued eventually.

Ezekiel's imagination became filled with visions of the many miraculous ways in which Yahweh would deliver Israel from Babylonian slavery and restore them to abundant blessings in the promised land. Yet, while the people would certainly enjoy all the promised benefits of God's future salvation, these promises came with one important proviso. Ezekiel explains:

> This is what the sovereign LORD says: It is not for your sake, O house of Israel, that I am going to do these things, but for the sake of my holy name, which you have profaned among the nations where you have gone. I will show the holiness of my great name, which has been profaned among the nations. (Ezek. 36:22–23 NIV)

Here is the Old Testament source for Jesus' teaching about prayer and the sanctification of God's name.

Yes, Yahweh will once again make a grand appearance on history's stage, similar to his awe-inspiriting performance at Mount Sinai long ago. God will again work marvels for the chosen people, rescuing them from Babylonian captivity, miraculously moving

---

4. Israel's profaning of God's name, and thus the importance of God reclaiming the sanctity of his name, is an important theme throughout the book of Ezekiel; see 13:19; 20:9, 14, 22; 22:26; 39:7.

the hearts and minds of hostile authorities, transforming their antagonism into active sympathy for Israel's plight. Israel will be allowed to return home. God will keep his covenant promises by blessing the people once again. And all the world will witness the power, mercy, and faithfulness of Yahweh.

Yet, Yahweh will be working primarily for himself. Divine *self*-exaltation, which is God's passion to reveal his majesty and to exalt himself before others, is a repeated refrain throughout the book of Ezekiel. It is the prerogative of divine holiness to expect and to seek public recognition. The fact that such self-seeking recognition does not accord with the human values of humility and meekness draws an important boundary line separating human understanding from divine realities. Ezekiel, or Yahweh speaking through Ezekiel, unashamedly declares:

> I had concern for my holy name, which the house of Israel profaned among the nations. (36:21)
>
> I will bring you against my land, O Gog, so that the nations may know me when I show myself holy through you. (38:16)
>
> I will show my greatness and my holiness, and I will make myself known in the sight of many nations. Then they will know that I am the LORD. (38:23)
>
> I will make known my holy name among my people. I will no longer let my holy name be profaned, and the nations will know that I the LORD am the Holy One in Israel. (39:7)
>
> I will display my glory among the nations. (39:21)
>
> I will be zealous for my holy name. (39:25)
>
> I will show myself holy through them in the sight of many nations. (39:27)

Notice that the Holy One is not above using others to accomplish the purposes of self-exaltation. When people behave this way, we avoid them and call them selfish. When God behaves this way, we bow down in worship and call him holy; we call him King of kings and Lord of lords. It marks out an important, challenging, and controversial line of separation between the worlds of holiness and not-holiness. We will need to explore these differences in the chapters ahead.

For now, it is enough to understand that God is a holy God. And it is in the nature of divine holiness not only to deserve public recognition but *to want* public recognition, to work for public recognition because that recognition is right and proper when the unholy creature stands before the holy Creator.

When God demands honor, he is doing nothing other than asking for what he deserves, what is his due. And we were made to do exactly this, to glorify our Creator. God will never receive all the applause that is rightfully his on this side of eternity. Thus, there will always be a deficit between the adoration God deserves and the glorification God's people are able to provide. Only when that public recognition is fully accomplished will we discover the ultimate purpose of our existence—understanding, of course, that even perfected humanity can never comprehend the full magnitude of God's glory.

Holiness and Salvation

There is one final point to make before drawing together the multicolored threads needed to complete the tapestry of what it means for God to sanctify his name.

It's a matter of timing.

In the book of Ezekiel, Yahweh is revealed as one to be respected, worshiped, and adored. Ezekiel also clarifies the process through which this goal is accomplished: it happens when Yahweh saves his covenant people, rescuing them from oppression, and establishing them in safety, peace, and security. In other words, God hallows his name by working out the miracle of salvation and giving people multiple stories to tell about the spectacular wonders that God has worked in their lives.

But when will this cosmic, God-glorifying rescue take place?

Ezekiel connects this vision of miraculous, wholesale rescue with God's promise of a new covenant and the gift of the Holy

Spirit. We find this idea expressed as well in Jeremiah 31:31–34, which specifically mentions the "new covenant."[5] Even though Ezekiel 36:24–28 lacks those two particular words; the prophet's vision aligns perfectly with Jeremiah's:

> For I will take you out of the nations; I will gather you from all the countries and bring you back into your own land. I will sprinkle clean water on you, and you will be clean; I will cleanse you from all your impurities and from all your idols. I will give you a new heart and put a new spirit in you; I will remove from you your heart of stone and give you a heart of flesh. And I will put my Spirit in you and move you to follow my decrees and be careful to keep my laws. Then you will live in the land I gave your ancestors; you will be my people, and I will be your God. (Ezek 36:24–28)

God exalts himself publicly and displays his holiness when universal salvation is finally accomplished; when he provides the gift of a Savior (Ezek 34:23–24; 37:22–25), the forgiveness of sins, the gift of the Holy Spirit, and the creation of a new, righteous humanity. Conversely, God also sanctifies his name when all those who reject his purposes and rebel against him suffer condemnation and punishment for their sinful rebellion.[6] No one exemplifies this alternative side of God's passion to reveal his holiness more forcefully than the godless nation of Gog, as described by Ezekiel 38:22–23. Against that nation the prophet warns:

> I will execute judgment on him with plague and bloodshed; I will pour down torrents of rain, hailstones and burning sulfur on him and on his troops and on the many nations with him. And so, I will show my greatness and my holiness, and I will make myself known in the sight of many nations. Then they will know that I am the LORD.

---

5. Jeremiah's description of the new covenant and its distinctives is discussed in the New Testament book of Hebrews 8:7–33. It is the longest Old Testament quotation in the New Testament.

6. For example, see Ezekiel 34:1–10, 17–22; 35:1–14; 36:1–7, 16–20.

When the heavenly curtain is finally pulled back and the brilliant beam of divine holiness blinds all, the pertinent question will be: who has seen God's holiness in their salvation, and who has experienced God's holiness in their condemnation?

Aligning Our Prayers with God's Priorities

So, to summarize what we've learned thus far:

Jesus teaches his disciples to pray, first and foremost, that our heavenly Father will glorify himself all throughout this world. *This should be every Christian's number one prayer request.* All Christian disciples can subject themselves to healthy self-examination in this regard, turning our hearts to a passionate concern for God's exaltation by setting aside our preoccupation with self-interest and personal problems. Such reflection helps us to realize that we are not the centerpiece of God's story. God is. And all of God's works, but especially Jesus' suffering on the cross, eventually point back to the Father and find their fulfillment in him as they glorify him.

The prophet Ezekiel teaches us that Yahweh's self-exaltation is a major concern in carving the channels and directing the flow of human history. God *will* sanctify his name with the assistance of human agency. Praying for God's glory to be sanctified in and through us is a request that God will always answer positively. This is the trajectory of Jesus' reliance on Ezekiel in the Lord's Prayer.

The centerpiece of our heavenly Father's self-glorification appears in the salvation of all his people. No one will be forgotten. None will be lost. Not a one can be taken out of his hands (John 10:28–29). God is especially glorified when recognized as the gracious savior God who is always faithful in keeping every promise.

Finally, this splendid combination of divine interest and achievement—that is, God's passion for his own self-glorification and the accomplishment of that glory—is ultimately unveiled in the final age when the Holy Spirit is poured out and the kingdom of God breaks through from heaven from earth. Jesus Christ inaugurated the new covenant through his blood shed on the cross; he also teaches us to pray for the fulfilment of that covenant when the

Father exalts himself as King of kings, Lord of lords, and the Savior of lost sinners, by saying, "Father, sanctify your Name."

Grasping something of the impenetrable mystery of God's holiness—what it means for God to be holy; and what it means for God's people to become holy—is the goal of this book. In one sense, it is an impossible task. In another sense, it is the most important of all necessary tasks.

Discussion Questions:

1. Restate in your own words the meaning of Jesus' request, "Father, hallowed be your name."
2. Why is it significant that Jesus makes this the *first* petition in this prayer?
3. What changes can you make in your prayer life to bring your prayers into greater conformity with Jesus' (and Ezekiel's) teaching about the sanctifying of God's name?

Chapter Two

The Holy, Wholly Other One

WHAT IS HOLINESS? WHAT does it mean to say Yahweh is a holy God?

There is a long Christian tradition of answering this question in one of two ways. The first identifies holiness with moral purity, ethical perfection. God is holy because God is supremely good and always does what is right. His character is the opposite of sin and wickedness. Moral perfection in thought, actions, and intentions is what makes God a holy God. By implication, it is also what makes God's people a holy people.

The second, related answer defines holiness in terms of separation. Holy people, as well as our holy God, are set apart, are sanctified from the imperfections of this fallen, unholy world. A holy God turns his back on wickedness, dissociating himself from every expression of sin or imperfection. God's holy people do the same. In this case, holiness means to be "in the world but not of the world." God and his people are made holy by not engaging with sin or having fellowship with sinners.

At times a decidedly negative aspect creeps into this second definition, placing a greater emphasis on what holiness is not rather than highlighting what holiness is. Thus, the second answer becomes related to the first. Yahweh's holiness is thought to consist in his perfect righteousness, and Yahweh's righteousness sets him apart from the rest of creation. Holiness consists in who we are not and what we do not do, e.g., smoke weed or consume sexually promiscuous entertainment.

As important as these two definitions are, however, with their emphases on being separated and set apart, neither of them takes us to the proper biblical starting point for understanding God's holiness. For holiness, in its most fundamental, biblical sense, is a matter of God's *Otherness*. In fact, God's holiness refers to the fact that God is *Wholly Other*, that is, utterly incomparable with everything. Before attempting a deeper explanation of what Wholly Other really means, let's take a look at this idea through the lens of a short Victorian novel called *Flatland*.

A Journey Through Flatland

Edwin A. Abbott (1838–1926) was a Church of England vicar and schoolmaster who published his small book *Flatland: A Romance of Many Dimensions* in 1884.[1] Abbott originally conceived of Flatland as a whimsical critique of the rigid, class-based hierarchies embedded within the social fabric of nineteenth-century Victorian society. Abbott's comical social commentary makes for an illuminating extended illustration for God's holiness, for him to be Wholly Other.

Within the storyline of Flatland, we find described two different, incompatible worlds: a two-dimensional world called Flatland and a three-dimensional world called Spaceland. Flatland is best compared to a vast sheet of paper. It consists of only two dimensions—length and width, with no height or depth. Flatland's residents were simple, geometrical figures like lines, squares, triangles, hexagons, and circles. Because Flatland had only two dimensions, its inhabitants knew nothing about cubes, cones, or spheres. In fact, any three-dimensional shape was virtually inconceivable to the resident of two-dimensional Flatland.

Flatland's two-dimensional realm shared its cosmos with a three-dimensional world called Spaceland. The residents of

1. Abbott, *Flatland*.

Hidden Holiness

Spaceland knew all about length and width, but more than this, they also experienced the third dimension, height or depth. In Spaceland, four-sided squares became six-sided cubes; triangles expanded into cones; and circles inflated into spheres. People in Spaceland actually inhabited the three-dimensional realities that those in Flatland could never even imagine.

A momentous event occurred in the history of Flatland the day it was visited by a resident from Spaceland. Let's call this visitor Mr. Ball. Mr. Ball was a large sphere who somehow managed to free himself from the boundaries of Spaceland. Being an adventurer at heart, Mr. Ball decided to introduce himself and to explore the neighboring two-dimensional realm of Flatland. But things didn't work out as he had hoped. Initially, the Flatlanders experienced Mr. Ball's introductions as a rather spooky, disembodied voice. They heard him shout, "Hello," from who knows where, but no one could see his figure.

Because two-dimensional Flatland lacked the capacity to contain a three-dimensional figure, it was impossible for Mr. Ball *to show* himself fully to its residents. Yet, Mr. Ball tried as best he could. He was determined to show himself to the people of Flatland within the constraints of Flatland's two-dimensional world. So, Mr. Ball entered Flatland and began to pass through it. At first, he miraculously appeared from nowhere as a single point, a dot that quickly morphed into a small circle. As Mr. Ball passed through Flatland, revealing more and more of himself, the circle grew in circumference until it was eventually quite large. Then the circle stopped growing and reversed course, diminishing in size, becoming smaller until it eventually shrunk into a tiny dot and vanished.

"There you have it!" shouted Mr. Ball's disembodied voice. "I have revealed all of myself to you in Flatland. Now do you understand what it means for me to live as a sphere in three dimensions?"[2]

Of course, the circles, squares, lines, and triangles of Flatland had all witnessed Mr. Ball's miraculous appearance, his expanding,

---

2. The imaginary dialogue is my addition to the story. It does not appear in the original.

shrinking, and disappearing circle. But this *revelation* brought them no closer to understanding what it meant for Mr. Ball to be a three-dimensional figure. In one sense they had encountered Mr. Ball, seeing him "through a glass darkly," so to speak (1 Cor 13:12 KJV). But, in another sense, the Flatlanders had not seen Mr. Ball at all; at least, not as he truly existed. The strange revelation was not sufficiently revelatory, not because Mr. Ball falsified any part of himself or held anything back, but because of the fundamental differences between the two realms. Only when (or if) the residents of Flatland were transported miraculously into the realm of Spaceland, where they could perceive three-dimensional creatures themselves, learning about length, width, and height from their own personal experience, only then might they be able to grasp something of Mr. Ball's spherical existence.

No illustration is perfect, of course. For instance, Mr. Ball is not Flatland's Creator. The Creator/creature distinction has no bearing on Mr. Ball's failure to reveal himself in Flatland. But the story of Flatland may, nevertheless, help us to understand two important issues at the heart of every discussion about the holiness of God, including why it is that grasping the meaning of holiness must be the starting point for understanding the God of the Bible.

Getting to Know the Infinite Qualitative Difference

The biblical God is essentially alien to our fallen humanity in this fallen world.[3] The differences separating Mr. Ball from the two-dimensional circles of Flatland are less than minuscule compared to the vast chasm separating the Holy One from his fallen creation. As Yahweh announces through the prophet Isaiah (55:8–9):

> "For my thoughts are not your thoughts,
>   neither are your ways my ways," declares the LORD.
> As the heavens are higher than the earth,

---

3. The incarnation of Jesus of Nazareth will cause us to reframe this statement. Yet, it does not make for a complete break between the Old and the New Testament perceptions of holiness. We will see that God's condescending grace is the unifying factor throughout the canon.

Hidden Holiness

so are my ways higher than your ways
and my thoughts than your thoughts."

Yahweh is fundamentally *un*like us in every way. God is eternal and uncreated, whereas we are mortal and created. God is infinite; we are finite. God is self-sustaining and defines himself; we are contingent creatures, dependent on others and our environment to determine our identity. Yes, God is personal, but God's personal attributes (traits like relationality, dependability, love, and wrath) are infinitely divine; whereas our personal attributes are not only limited by our creatureliness, they are also marred and made dysfunctional by our sinfulness. In this way, human beings face a double impediment when it comes to knowing their Creator.

There are two Christian thinkers we will learn from who have made this infinite chasm between the holy God and fallen humanity a special focus of their theological writings: Søren Kierkegaard (1813–1855) and Karl Barth (1886–1968). We will get to Barth later in the chapter. Kierkegaard was a brilliant Danish Christian writer who described the unimaginably vast distinction between the infinite, uncreated Creator and his finite, created creatures as the *Infinite Qualitative Difference*. This chasm is a fundamental, nonnegotiable condition that is defined by God as God, the holy One.

Kierkegaard described the central subject matter of theology—that is, the investigation of God and God's relationship with humanity—as "the ultimate paradox." Since God is infinitely unlike humanity, and since no one can imagine or understand something that is infinitely different from himself, anyone who imagines that he can reason his way to understanding God is trying "to discover something that thought itself cannot think."[4] This paradox demonstrates why God can only be understood through divine revelation:[5]

---

4. Kierkegaard, *Philosophical Fragments*, 37; chapter 3 is devoted to "The Absolute Paradox."

5. Kierkegaard, *Philosophical Fragments*, 35, 45, 46–47.

The Holy, Wholly Other One

> This then is the ultimate paradox of thought: to want to discover something that thought itself cannot think . . . Defined as the absolutely different, it [God] seems to be at the point of being disclosed, but not so, because the understanding cannot even think the absolutely different . . . At this point we seem to stand at a paradox. Just to come to know that the god is the different, man needs the god and comes to know that the god is absolutely different from him.

We tend to imagine God in terms of extended analogies based on human qualities or some feature of creation. We assume that being made in God's image (Gen 1:27), human beings can now serve as a reliable, finite model for God's personhood—in other words, since we are like "this," we may deduce that God is like "*This*."

Kierkegaard insists that this method is a colossal mistake arguing that, barring a miraculous act by God himself, the gulf separating creature from Creator is infinite and unbridgeable. Human beings can never discover the truth about God on their own. It is impossible for us to reach out and touch the Creator from our side of the infinite, qualitative divide. In extolling the transcendent power and majesty of Yahweh, the book of Job confirms Kierkegaard's point by also asserting that God is far beyond human comprehension. "Surely God is great, *and we do not know him*; the number of his years is unsearchable" (Job 36:26). Even in *knowing* God we must confess that *we really do not know him at all*. Yahweh is too great for us to grasp. Consequently, knowing God can only be a gift that God bestows. We are entirely dependent on God's gracious willingness to reach down, to touch us and show himself to us. And even in receiving that gift of revelation, we still do not really *know* the holy One as he is in himself.

Further Biblical Reflection on God's Infinite Qualitative Difference

This gulf between Creator and creature is not only an aspect of God being infinite, there is also a qualitative dimension to the gulf between us and our creator. A *quantitative* gulf can conceivably be bridged by adding something more: more time, more effort, more prayer, more knowledge, more righteousness, a greater quantity of something that could bring humanity into contact with the Creator. However, a *qualitative* gulf is a difference in kind. Think of the distinction between oil and water, between chalk and cheese. Or better yet, think of the difference between the animate and the inanimate, a living creature over and against a cold hard rock. Each is qualitatively different, fundamentally unlike the other. They will always remain essentially separate and distinct. The one can never cross over and become the same as the other. So, even though Mr. Ball visits Flatland and *reveals* himself, it remains impossible for two-dimensional figures to grasp his three-dimensional existence.

However, these comparisons remain grossly inadequate. For oil and water, chalk and cheese, and living things and rocks are still very much alike in important ways. They are each composed of matter. They are all tangible. They can be measured and weighed. God, however, is neither measurable nor quantifiable. God is not a substance. God is immeasurable, immaterial, unquantifiable, eternal Spirit.

This unbridgeable gulf ever persists between the Infinite, Qualitatively Different, Wholly Other, creator God, on the one hand, and all finite, fallen, created things, on the other. Grappling with this distinction is the starting point for understanding the essence of divine holiness in the Bible. There is nothing else and no one else like Yahweh, the God and Father of our Lord Jesus Christ. There is no category of *god-ness* by which Yahweh may be compared to other gods, goddesses, or divine spirits. God exists in a category of One because Yahweh is the one and the only God. Both the Old and the New Testaments testify to God's thoroughgoing uniqueness:

The Holy, Wholly Other One

> How great you are Sovereign LORD! There is no one like you, and there is no God but you, as we have heard with our own ears. (2 Sam 7:22)
>
> O LORD Almighty, God of Israel, enthroned between the cherubim, you alone are God over all the kingdoms of the earth. You have made heaven and earth. (Isa 37:16)
>
> Now to the King eternal, immortal, invisible, the only God, be honor and glory for ever and ever. Amen. (1 Tim 1:17)

Biblically speaking, to say that God is holy is another way of saying that God is God, the one and only God. This is also why the Old Testament prophets identify Yahweh as "the Holy One." In Amos 4:2 the prophet announces that "the Sovereign LORD has sworn by his holiness," which is merely another way of saying that "the Sovereign LORD has sworn by himself" (Amos 6:8). The prophet Habakkuk prays for the people of Israel saying, "God came from Teman, the Holy One from Mount Paran. His glory covered the heavens and his praise filled the earth" (Hab 3:3; also see Isa 55:5). Yahweh is "the high and lofty One who lives in a high and holy place; he lives forever, whose name is holy" (Isa 57:15).

As a result, because God is the Holy One, the divine attributes such as love, mercy, righteousness, or wrath are all qualified by holiness. It is false simply to imagine God's attributes as perfected versions of human attributes. God's love is not a bigger, expanded perfected version of human love. This would be to view the differences in merely quantitative terms.[6] But the real difference is divine holiness, the infinite qualitative difference. God exhibits only holy love, holy mercy, holy righteousness, and holy wrath. In the words of theologian John Webster:[7]

---

6. The Old Testament scholar Gerhard von Rad puts is like this: "The holy is the primeval religious datum; that is, the concept of the holy cannot in any way be deduced from other human standards of value. It is not their elevation to the highest degree, nor is it associated with them by way of addition. The holy could much more aptly be designated the great stranger in the human world . . . it is, in fact, the 'wholly other'"; *Old Testament Theology*, 1.205.

7. Webster, *Holiness*, 43.

> Holiness is the decisive attribute for knowing and acknowledging God and for understanding his will and action; on this... all other knowledge of the attributes of God depends. If the holiness of God is not perceived and understood, then the entire work and conduct of God are not grasped.

Only insofar as these attributes express the Infinite Qualitative Difference of divine holiness are they genuine expressions of God's character.

God's Revelation Is Always True but Not Exhaustive

Another issue that arises when grappling with the nature of God's Wholly Otherness is that God's self-revelation will never be exhaustive. Everything that God shows us of himself will always be true; he never misleads or deceives us. Because God is infinitely and qualitatively different from all his creation, we can never see or know or understand everything that there is to see or to know or to understand about God. God is essentially holy. This cannot be said about any part of creation, including human beings. In this sense, any self-revelation God may offer to us will always remain partial—reliable and adequate for our salvation, but far from comprehensive. There will always be something more to see and apprehend, including the fact that God is forever mysterious and beyond our apprehension.

Think again of Mr. Ball's entrance, his *revelation*, if you will, into the world of Flatland. Mr. Ball revealed himself to the fullest extent possible within a two-dimensional world. The residents of Flatland saw everything they could possibly see of Mr. Ball. Yet, the revelation fell far short of the ultimate reality. An expanding and shrinking circle, beginning and ending with a dot, is not the same thing as a sphere. The two-dimensional creatures were simply incapable of grasping a three-dimensional reality because that reality transcends the boundaries of two-dimensional life. That is an unbridgeable, qualitative difference created by God's holiness.

The Holy, Wholly Other One

Karl Barth and the Wholly Other

The Swiss theologian Karl Barth is the other theologian mentioned above that focused a good deal of attention on the Wholly Otherness of God. Elaborating on the important ideas found in Job 36:26: "Surely God is great, and we do not know him; the number of his years is unsearchable," Barth considered that the separation between God and humanity is so unimaginably vast that the Holy One remains hidden even in his revelation. God's inevitable mystery and hiddenness is the essence of divine holiness. Barth puts it like this:[8]

> But we ourselves have no capacity for fellowship with God. Between God and us there stands the hiddenness of God, in which He is far from us and foreign to us except as He has of Himself ordained and created fellowship between Himself and us—and this does not happen in the actualizing of our capacity, but in the miracle of His good-pleasure . . God is known only by God; God can be known only by God. At this very point, in faith itself, we know God in utter dependence, in discipleship and gratitude . . . In faith itself we are forced to say that our knowledge of God begins in all seriousness with the knowledge of the hiddenness of God.

Scripture affirms Barth's insight by pointing towards this holy dynamic of divine hiddenness in a variety of ways. Remember that Yahweh threatens "to break out" against his people and to destroy them if they approach too closely or fail to consecrate themselves properly at Mt. Sinai (Exod 19:22, 24). As Yahweh descended to the foot of Mt. Sinai, the entire mountain was covered with a thick cloud. The smoke became more and more intense as Yahweh descended on it "with fire. The smoke billowed up like smoke from a furnace" (Exod 19:18), ensuring that as Yahweh revealed himself the Israelites could see nothing. When Moses requested a special revelation for himself, Yahweh warned, "You cannot see my face, for no one may see me and live" (Exod 33:20). The people of Beth

---

8. Barth, *Church Dogmatics*, 2.1, 182.

Hidden Holiness

Shemesh experience this lesson the hard way when many of them died after looking into the ark of the covenant. The people cried out with horror, "Who can stand in the presence of the LORD, this holy God?" (1 Sam 6:20).

Even as the Gospel of John insists that the Old Testament warnings about the dangers of seeing God have been overcome in Jesus Christ (John 1:18), the Infinite Qualitative Difference continues to hide God in his holiness. The apostle Paul reminded Timothy that the Father of Jesus Christ was "the King of Kings and Lord of Lords, who alone is immortal and who lives in unapproachable light, whom no one has seen or can see" (1 Tim 6:15–16). The writer to the Hebrews reminds his readers that God's judgment always begins with his own people. "The LORD will judge his people. It is a dreadful thing to fall into the hand of the living God" (Heb. 10:30–31). Without any threat of judgment, Hebrews 12:28 describes the dread and awe most appropriate for meeting the Father when he arrives in his kingdom: "Since we are receiving a kingdom that cannot be shaken, let us be thankful, and so worship God acceptably with reverence and awe, for our God is a consuming fire." This God can be greeted in one way and one way only: in abject humility with the fear of the LORD.

Perceiving the chasm between God and us, which is the Infinite Qualitative Difference, remains a revelatory blessing, just as being allowed to glimpse beyond it remains an awe-inspiring danger, for God ever remains as hidden in his revelation as his revelation is illuminated in his hiddenness. Even the believer's forgiveness and acceptance in Jesus Christ cannot soften the terrible spiritual shock awaiting every sinner (redeemed or not) brought into the eternal presence of the Holy One. For believers, this meeting ought to be met with joy and thanksgiving even as it will be met in fear and trembling.

Discussion Questions:

1. In your own words, explain the meaning of the phrase "the infinite qualitative difference." What does this infinite

qualitative difference have to do with understanding God's holiness?

2. What is the hiddenness of God? How can God remain hidden from us even as God reveals himself to us? Isn't this a contradiction? How does this concept add to our understanding of God's holiness?

3. How do these concepts influence or shape our worship and adoration of our holy God?

Chapter Three

Seeing the Invisible, Knowing the Unknowable God

MY YEARS OF SEMINARY training in Vancouver, British Columbia provided one of the most enjoyable, productive periods of my young Christian life. I felt like a hog in slop wallowing among more fecund opportunities to learn and to grow in my relationship with Christ and my understanding of God's word than I could ever have imagined. Every discovery offered another opportunity to draw closer to my Savior.

Being an avid reader of all my professors' suggested reading lists led me down delightfully unexpected rabbit trails in the recesses of the seminary's library. One of those rabbit trails led me to the strange work of a German theologian named Louis Karl Rudolf Otto (1869–1909). That work was Otto's much discussed book, *The Idea of the Holy*.[1] It grabbed me by the heart and mind and has never let go. This was not because the book was particularly brilliant (not all have found it so) but because Otto's insights helped me to begin to grasp something about my God and God's revelation. Otto was the first to help me realize that in and of

---

1. The original German title is simply *The Holy* published in 1917; the English translation is *The Idea of the Holy*.

Seeing the Invisible, Knowing the Unknowable God

himself, *God is Wholly Other*, the infinite majestic mystery far beyond human comprehension.[2]

Otto's insight into the Otherness of our Creator marked the trailhead of wisdom in my understanding, because such wisdom is also the beginning of the "fear of the Lord" (Prov 1:7). Never mind that *The Idea of the Holy* is "probably the most widely read theological work in German of the twentieth century."[3] Never mind that "the history of the concept of holiness in the twentieth century cannot be comprehended without reference to *The Idea of the Holy*."[4] Rudolf Otto was an academic who wrote with the passion of one who was humbly yet intensely seeking after God in his own life. Raised in a deeply pious, Lutheran household, Otto was steeped in the Scriptures from an early age. Those biblical harmonies provided the context for all of his work in comparative religion. Otto translates the theological conclusions which he draws from Scripture into psychological observations drawn from religious experience. This comes across most especially in his identification of God as Wholly Other.

During a 1911 trip throughout North Africa and Asia, Otto attended a Moroccan synagogue service in the early spring.[5] In detailing the "dark and inconceivably grimy" walls of the ancient structure in one of his letters, Otto also attended to the Hebrew liturgical chants and Scripture readings during the service in the candle-lit cavern. He found himself overwhelmed by the reading of Isaiah 6 extolling the Holy One seated on his heavenly throne:

> . . . suddenly out of the babel of voices, causing a thrill of fear, there it begins, unified, clear and unmistakable: . . . *Holy, Holy, Holy, Lord God of Hosts, the heavens and the earth are full of thy glory* . . . these most exalted words that have ever come from human lips always grip one

---

2. See chapter 2 of this book.

3. Crowder, "Rudolf Otto's *The Idea of the Holy* Revisited," 22; quoting Hans Zahrnt.

4. Crowder, "Rudolf Otto's *The Idea of the Holy* Revisited," 24.

5. For Otto's description of his synagogue experience, see Almond, *Rudolf Otto*, 17–18.

in the depths of the soul, with a mighty shudder exciting and calling into play the mystery of the other world latent therein.

Grasping Holiness Does Not Begin with Ethics

I discussed in chapter 2 that understanding God as *Wholly Other* is the starting point for understanding God's holiness. This insight is Otto's crucial contribution to biblical theology and interpretation. Holiness is not, first or foremost, a moral quality.[6] It is not principally about ethics. We have a crucial stretch of theological road to travel first before we can add this secondary, ethical sense to our understanding of holiness. It is true that the Hebrew word for holiness, *qadosh*, is frequently defined in terms of "separation" or being "set apart."[7] Yet, we must ask the question, who or what is separated or set apart from who or what? It is a long-standing mistake to assume that the idea of "separation" must always be filled exclusively with priestly type concepts such as set apart from impurity, separated from uncleanness, from the profane or immoral.

We have seen that the more fundamental meaning of holiness *describes the Creator as separated from all of creation*, not only because that creation has fallen into sin, but more fundamentally, because creation is utterly dependent upon and distinct from its Creator. Though creation depends upon God for its existence, there is no point where God's being is limited or defined by his creation. There is no bridge that inherently leads from one to the other. The two are separated by an Infinite Qualitative Difference.[8] Even God's relationship with human beings reveals this difference.

---

6. Brünner, *Christian Doctrine of God*, 165; Otto, *Idea of the Holy*, 52. Brünner's book draws from Otto's work. Brünner writes, "'The Holy', as Rudolf Otto's beautiful book has shown us in an impressive and conclusive manner, is that to which the religious act is directed. Holiness is the very nature of [God]" (157).

7. For discussions about the usage of both the Hebrew and Greek words for holy/holiness see, Harrington, *Holiness*, 11–44; Hodgson Jr., "Holiness (NT)," 249–54; Wright, "Holiness (OT)," 237–49.

8. See the previous chapter.

Seeing the Invisible, Knowing the Unknowable God

Humans, in all of creation, are most aptly compared to God by way of analogy as those created "in God's image." In actuality, they too demonstrate the infinite chasm separating their creatureliness from the Holy One. For in every way that human beings may resemble God, they yet remain absolutely unlike God.[9] Each and every resemblance to God is a gift from their Creator.

Had God never decided to reveal himself to the world, we could never know anything about God's holiness, for we can only know God through his self-revelation. We only see what God shows us. We only grasp what God gives us the means to grasp. Even if creation's beauty moves us to posit the existence of a beautiful Creator (Rom 1:18–20), our hypotheses about this theoretical Creator would never move beyond the realm of childish imaginations and simple guesswork.

The Dialectical Tension of Personal Relationship

We can see that God's holiness generates an immense tension, a dialectical tension, each end pulling against the other—both sides being true, but both in need of explanation by the other. This tension arises the moment an individual comes into contact with the Holy One.

Like a small child mesmerized by the dancing yellow and red flames of a campfire, human beings are both attracted and threatened by the holiness of God. Holiness is both beautiful and dangerous, destroying anyone who approaches too closely or carelessly. "The holiness of God thus involves peril to the man with whom He has fellowship."[10] This is one side of the dialectical tension. God's holiness, like a burning fire, quickly warns those

---

9. "Man (sic) is absolutely unlike God in the fact that his (sic) creative activity is always connected to that which is *given* him (sic) . . . In all that makes man like God, man remains absolutely unlike Him, in that fact that all that he has, he has received from God and that for all that he does he is responsible, so that his very freedom can only be realized in absolute obedience to God"; Brünner, *Christian Doctrine of God*, 177.

10. Barth, *Church Dogmatics* 2.1, 364.

Hidden Holiness

who would draw near to stand back in holy fear. Intimacy without God's accommodation to us is impossible. To quote Otto:[11]

> The truly mysterious object [God] is beyond our apprehension and comprehension, not only because our knowledge has certain irremovable limits, but because in it we come upon something inherently wholly other, whose kind and character are incommensurable with our own, and before which we therefore *recoil in a wonder that strikes us chill and numb.*

The holiness of God "evokes an incomparable sense of distance from Him (sic). God in his nature is inaccessible. He dwells in light unapproachable."[12] To sense God's holiness is to understand how very, very far away we are from him. When Moses caught a glimpse of the mysteriously burning bush in Exodus 3, he was confronted by the mesmerizing, enigmatic, irresistible beauty in the divine fire. The burning bush communicated Yahweh's majesty to Moses. Initially, he is drawn to that divine fire like iron shavings to a magnet. We can comprehend Moses' attraction as human fascination with the other. However, Moses is stopped in his tracks when God reveals a little more of himself until he is quickly pinned to the (holy) ground like a moth anesthetized and added to God's collection. When Moses heard God's voice, he "hid his face, because he was afraid to look at God" (verse 6). He drew back, recoiling in fear and trepidation with an overwhelming wonder that struck him "chill and numb." Moses' limited creatureliness is frozen under the divine gaze of the Wholly Other.

The context of Exodus 3 shows us that holiness is the overwhelming mystery of God that attracts but ultimately repels as it is so overwhelming. Like Moses, we too are fascinated, drawn inexorably to God's irresistible brilliance while simultaneously warned to halt and stand back, even to hide ourselves, for our own safety. No created thing is fit to approach the Holy One on its own.

Perhaps Isaiah's vision of the heavenly throne room (6:1–8) is the most well-known instance of someone *seeing* God's holiness

11. Otto, *Idea of the Holy*, 28.
12. Brünner, *Christian Doctrine of God*, 162.

while teetering on the precipice of annihilation. Overwhelmed by the angels' song, "Holy, holy, holy is the Lord God almighty," the prophet prostrates himself on the floor and cries out, "Woe is me! I am undone . . . for my eyes have seen the King, the Lord of hosts." Isaiah recognizes that facing the holy One could be his undoing.

A closer reading, however, reveals that there is a dialectic, an inherent biblical tension, in play when it comes to God and his holiness. On the one hand, no one can see God and live. On the other, Scripture assures us that the holy One is also the God who wants to reveal his holiness; he wants the "whole world to be filled with his glory" (Ps 72:19). Yahweh is a God of revelation *who wants to be known*, wants to be seen, wants to walk in relationship with all those willing to respond to his self-disclosure in faith and obedience. Another aspect of God's Otherness presents itself to us here. God's holiness includes both *the will* to reveal himself and *the concern* for personal relationship. Consequently, the infinite measure of God's holiness becomes the infinite measure of God's desire both to know and to be known by human beings. The revelation that confirms the infinite distance between Creator and creature is the same revelation that overcomes that gulf by making God known.[13]

Returning again to Exodus 3, at the very moment Moses "hid his face because he was afraid to look at God, the LORD said to him, 'I have indeed seen the misery of my people in Egypt. I have heard them crying out because of their slave drivers, and I am concerned about their suffering. So, I have come down to rescue them from the hand of the Egyptians'" (Exod 3:6–8). This passage perfectly captures the significance of holiness understood as integral to God's will and desire. It appears in the apparent dialectical tension between God's hiddenness, on the one hand, and God's desire for relationship with his people, on the other. The holy One's presence *remains dangerous* even as Yahweh promises *to bring salvation* for the people of Israel.

---

13. See Brünner, *Christian Doctrine of God*, 163.

Hidden Holiness

Unveiling the Dangerous Redeemer in the Ultimate Dialectic

The theologian Emil Brünner describes the tension between God's dangerous and consuming holiness and God's relational nature as "the ultimate dialectic."[14] As the ultimate dialectic, it reveals the Holy One to be *a dangerous Redeemer*: *dangerous* due to the Infinite Qualitative Difference; a *Redeemer* because of the Holy One's infinite concern to enter into personal relationship. Forging this paradoxical connection is an important theme in the second half of the book of Isaiah. In fact, this duality in God is expressed in a new way as Israel's God is described in Isaiah as "the LORD, your Redeemer, the Holy One of Israel."[15]

On the one hand, as the *Holy One* of Israel, Yahweh (the LORD) has sent his people, Israel, into Babylonian captivity, reminding them of how seriously they had transgressed the terms of the Sinai covenant. This reveals how Yahweh takes himself, his holiness, his relationships, and his promises very seriously. The Holy One will not be ignored, much less exploited. Israel faced the consequences of its rebellion.

On the other hand, as the *Holy Redeemer* of Israel, Yahweh still promises to bless the nation and restore its fortunes by rescuing them from captivity. Neither theme, of punishment or rescue, is ever far from the other in Isaiah. The promises of future redemption are always conditioned by prophetic reminders of the terms of God's covenant: absolute obedience to Yahweh's will.

Relationship with the Holy One always comes with demands even as it is gracious. Yes, Yahweh desires relationship with his people, but Yahweh strictly defines the terms of that relationship. Violating Yahweh's expressed will can literally amount to a death sentence. We have already seen divinely established boundaries laid out in Exodus chapters 3:5–6 (Moses is warned to avoid holy ground and becomes afraid to look at God) and 19:10–13, 22–24

---

14. Brünner, *Christian Doctrine of God*, 163.
15. See Isaiah 41:14; 43:3; 47:4; 48:17; 49:7; 54:5.

(people are put to death for touching Mount Sinai; the LORD warns that he may "break out against" the people who transgress).

Yahweh decides *who* is allowed to approach him in his holiness (Moses, Aaron, priests); *how* they may approach (with special clothing, purification rituals, sacrifices); and *how near* they may be allowed to approach God's presence (the foot of the mountain, not the summit; the outer court vs. the inner court of the tabernacle). Anyone who violates the rules expressed by Yahweh is struck dead by the Holy One himself.[16] These reactions are not fits of anger but demonstrate God's holiness and the Infinite Qualitative Difference separating creature and Creator.

Aaron, Moses' brother, witnessed his own sons Nadab and Abihu perish as they violated God's instructions on burning incense. "They offered unauthorized fire before the LORD, contrary to his command. So, fire came out from the presence of the LORD and consumed them, and they died before the LORD" (Lev 10:1–2). Yahweh explained through Moses:

> "'Among those who approach me
> I will show myself holy;
> in the sight of all the people
> I will be honored.'" (verse 3)

These Scriptures attest to the seriousness with which the Holy One defends his holiness. In showing himself to be holy the Infinite Qualitative Difference is on full display for us. God reaches across that difference in his revelation of himself. Even as he does so, God reminds his people that he remains still Wholly Other, unlike them in every way. Failure to stand in awe of God's holiness is playing with holy fire from the Wholly Other, and God shows himself ready to defend his holiness even with terrible and deadly results. Recall that God declares his intent "to show himself holy in the sight of all the people" (Ezek 26: 23). Recall as well that this is also the prayer request every disciple ought to pray for, according to the Lord's Prayer.[17]

---

16. See Exodus 19:12, 22, 24.
17. See chapter 1.

This fearful expression of God's own holiness is found throughout our Scriptures. After the Israelites destroyed the city of Jericho (Josh 6), an Israelite warrior, Achan, hoarded some of the spoils of war for himself, defying the Lord's command to destroy what spoils were not devoted to the tabernacle treasury, in other words, all of the city's valuables (6:17–27). When Achan is found out, he is stoned and his body burned (verses 25–26). Yahweh had warned, "He who is caught with devoted things shall be destroyed by fire . . . He has violated the covenant of the Lord" (verse 15).

Another similarly weighty story is found in 2 Samuel when king David moved the ark of the covenant, the throne of Yahweh's glory, to the city of Jerusalem. A well-meaning, pious man named Uzzah died for trying to avert catastrophe. "When they came to the threshing floor of Nakon, Uzzah reached out and took hold of the ark of God, because the oxen stumbled. The Lord's anger burned against Uzzah because of his irreverent act; therefore, God struck him down, and he died there beside the ark of God" (2 Sam 6:6–7).

If space permitted, these biblical examples could be multiplied several times over. And this dangerous dimension of God's holiness is not restricted to the Old Testament. Although there is definitely a shift that comes with the new covenant, examples persist of the Holy One continuing to reveal himself as the *dangerous Redeemer* in the New Testament, as well.

Our Dangerous Redeemer in the New Testament

Jesus is very clear when he describes how small is the gate and how narrow is the road leading into the kingdom of God. So much so that he warns "only a few will find it" (Matt 7:13–14). Jesus describes himself as "the Way, the Truth, and the Life," warning anyone who will listen that "no one comes to the Father except through me" (John 14:6). The message is clear: no one approaches the Father's throne under their own power, according to their own plan, via their own means or methods. God continues to take the boundaries of holiness very seriously. The threat meant to evoke holy fear is that on judgment day many will hear Jesus' final words to them: "Get away from me you evildoers. I never knew you" (Matt 7:23).

Jesus may appear meek at times, but he is seldom mild. Threats of future judgment appear throughout the four Gospels, but especially in the Synoptics.[18] Listeners are warned to "produce fruit in keeping with repentance . . . The ax is already at the root of the trees, and every tree that does not produce good fruit will be cut down and thrown into the fire" (Luke 3:8–9). The earthly Jesus gave far more attention to warnings about impending judgment, and teaching about how to avoid it, than he did consoling his listeners with promises of divine love. In fact, "the Synoptics record Jesus saying well over twice as much about the wrath of God as he ever did about his love."[19] The dangerous Old Testament encounters with the Holy One, Israel's Redeemer, the God who is Wholly Other, resonate loudly as the theological background to the numerous examples of threat and warning in Jesus' teaching and the rest of the New Testament.

The early church had its own stories to tell illustrating the dangers of ignoring the Holy One's boundaries and laws. In Acts 5:1–11 Ananias conspires with his wife Sapphira to pull the wool over the eyes of the Holy Spirit—as if they could keep anything secret from the Creator who is Wholly Other. When the apostle Peter confronts them with their sin, they both instantly "fell down and died" (verses 6, 10). Their deaths offered a dramatic reminder to the nascent church regarding the fearful holy God they were dealing with.

Similarly, the apostle Paul taught the church in Corinth about the sanctity of the Lord's Supper, warning church members to search themselves, to repent and confess their sins ahead of time so that they will not "eat the bread or drink the cup of the Lord in an unworthy manner." Anyone who participates casually or unseriously "eats and drinks judgment on himself. That is why many

---

18. Matthew, Mark, and Luke.

19. See Lane, "Wrath of God," 150. Lane is quoting J. A. Baird, *Justice of God in the Teaching of Jesus*, 59–60, 72.

among you [the Corinthians] are weak and sick, and a number of you have died" (1 Cor 11:27–30). Church members were neglecting God's requirements for the Lord's Supper. In creating obstacles for others approaching God's holy presence, their judgment was as tangible as disease and death.

The Holy One's warnings about the need to pay proper attention to the way in which he is approached are as important today as they were for Moses, Achan, Isaiah, Uzzah, Ananias, Sapphira, and the Corinthian church. They literally remain a matter of eternal life and death. The heavenly Father has not changed; he remains the same as he has ever been. There is no difference between the Old Testament and the New Testament in this regard. Yahweh's self-disclosure as the Holy One, the dangerous Redeemer, the One who is Wholly Other, whose revelation measures God's infinite desire for intimacy even as it demonstrates the Infinite Qualitative Difference between creature and Creator, is as relevant after Christ's advent as it was before.

Understanding God's Love Through Holiness

I understand that these observations will cut against the grain of much modern theology, both popular and academic. For some, these biblical stories and their explanations I offer will be highly offensive. Modern folk prefer to emphasize God's love and mercy over and above God's wrath, judgment, or jealousy. This is one of the more common ways in which we try to domesticate God, keeping him confined within humanly approved boundaries amenable to modern sensibilities. But how can the Holy One ever be domesticated? The Holy One will forever remain a cause for offense as the Wholly Other.

We need the proper approach if we are to gain a proper appreciation of God's love. If we are to have an adequate measure of understanding of God's love, we cannot take shortcuts. We must begin with God's holiness if we are to understand how and why God's love must be grasped as *holy love* offered by the One who is

Wholly Other. Rudolph Otto remarked on this issue when commenting on the jolting nature of divine judgment:[20]

> [Judgment is] a moment whose singularly daunting and awe-inspiring character must be gravely disturbing to those persons who will recognize nothing in the divine nature but goodness, gentleness, love, and a sort of confidential intimacy, in a word, only those aspects of God which turn towards the world of men.

For some readers it surely will be disturbing and offensive to hear that our Redeemer is also dangerous; that we can only begin to understand God's love in relation to God's holiness because holiness is the infinite measure of divine love. Yes, the Holy One does graciously turn towards the world to rescue and redeem sinners, *but only as the Holy One.*

Discussion Questions:

1. This chapter argues that a proper understanding of God's holiness cannot begin with a discussion of ethics or morality. What is meant by this and why is it important?
2. What does it mean to describe God as Wholly Other? Why is this central to a proper understanding of God's holiness?
3. What is meant by the term "ultimate dialectic" and how does this relate to both the Father's and the Son's status as a "dangerous Redeemer"?
4. How might these ideas influence our own understanding of worship, prayer and our life in Christ?

---

20. Otto, *Idea of the Holy,* 19.

Chapter Four

The Problem with "the Problem" of Divine Violence

DISCOVERING THAT GOD CAN be offensive and grappling with the mystery of God's holiness is a strange and unappealing process for some. For those who have been inattentive to this part of the Bible's narrative, the Holy One can appear unfair and cruel. If we consider God in his dangerous holiness as we might judge our fellow human beings, then certainly, God may appear cruel to us. But it will be helpful in addressing this question to begin with the apostle Paul's Letter to the Romans.

In the New Testament book of Romans chapter 9, Paul attempts to answer a question he must have heard frequently: if Jesus Christ is the Jewish messiah, why have so many Jews failed to believe in him? Jewish Christians were (and are) a small minority in the Jewish community. Why is this? Paul sought to answer the criticism that this fact amounted to a compelling argument against the truth of the gospel. After all, shouldn't we expect the majority of Jews to recognize their own messiah?

Paul begins to answer this question with a discussion of how the sovereign God chooses or, in theological parlance, elects those who wound up as giants in the biblical story (Rom 9:1–21). Beginning with Abraham's sons, God chose Isaac but not Ishmael to receive God's covenant blessings (verses 6–9). In the next generation,

The Problem with "the Problem" of Divine Violence

God chose Jacob but not Esau (verses 10–13). God elected Isaac and Jacob for his own holy purposes, not because of anything good or bad they had done, but simply because they were the ones he wanted to choose (verse 11–12).

Paul then raises the next obvious question: "What then shall we say? Is God unjust?" (verse 14).

Let's face it. Paul's description of divine election sounds, to modern ears, more than unjust; it sounds downright barbaric. It appears to be arbitrary, callous, manipulative, and worst of all, unloving. This is not the kind of behavior one would expect from a gracious, kind, and merciful God, which is the preferred image of God for most people today. Yet, God says, "Jacob I loved, but Esau I hated" (verse 13b), a divine decision made while the twins were still in their mother's womb!

Paul does not appear to be helping his cause at this point. In fact, many listeners would say that he is digging himself into a deeper and deeper hole. I can easily imagine some of his non-Jewish audience walking away, turning their backs as they say, "If this is the kind of God you serve, count me out. I don't want anything to do with him." Today, many Bible readers are prone to say similar things when encountering such passages.

Yet, rather than softening his words, or amending his argument in a more palatable tone, Paul doubles down on his point:

> What then shall we say? Is God unjust? Not at all! For he says to Moses,
>
> "I will have mercy on whom I have mercy,
>   and I will have compassion on whom I have compassion."
>
> It does not, therefore, depend on human desire or effort, but on God's mercy . . . Therefore, God has mercy on whom he wants to have mercy, and he hardens whom he wants to harden. (verses 14–15, 18)

The problem is obvious: How do we avoid the verdict that God is, in fact, unjust when the application of divine mercy appears whimsical? But Paul does not appear interested in winning this argument. In fact, he becomes increasingly offensive to those who find such reasoning difficult, and seems to have given his listeners another excellent reason to reject his gospel. Notice that he does not really answer the question he raises; he merely denies its implication about God's apparent injustice. Somehow or another, the idea that God shows mercy to whomever he chooses—and by implication withholds mercy from those he chooses to harden—is taken as an adequate response to his opponents' objection:

> One of you will say to me: "Then why does God still blame us? For who is able to resist his will?" But who are you, a human being, to talk back to God? "Shall what is formed say to the one who formed it, 'Why did you make me like this?'" Does not the potter have the right to make out of the same lump of clay some pottery for special purposes and some for common use? (verses 19–21)

Paul brings down the curtain on this debate by declaring God's sovereign right to do as he pleases. Is Paul being glib or insensitive? No, he is only writing as a believer in the God of the biblical stories he relays, and as the Bible can be offensive to human ears, so Paul can sound offensive in this epistle.

"Who in the blazes are you?" Paul asks. "Who are you to talk back to God, to question his decisions?" Some will say that Paul is now arguing in bad faith, making a power play to shut down his opponent. Yet, whether we like it or not, this is the apostle's answer. Doesn't the Holy One, the Creator, the sovereign ruler who is Wholly Other, the one who is separated from us by an Infinite Qualitative Difference, doesn't this infinite God have not only the freedom but the right to work in human history as he chooses, whether or not we are able to understand it? Throughout this bird's eye view of God's history of choosing people for his own purposes, God demonstrates divine wrath, power, patience, and mercy in order to magnify "the riches of his glory" (verses 22–23).

We are reminded again that the Holy One ultimately works for his own glorification. It is God's right to glorify himself as he chooses, for God alone is holy.

The Problem with "the Problem" of Divine Violence

Then, to make sure that we do not miss his point, Paul closes the more extended section of his argument in chapters ten and eleven with this doxology (11:33–36):

> Oh, the depth of the riches of the wisdom and knowledge of God!
>> How unsearchable his judgments,
>> and his paths beyond tracing out!
> "Who has known the mind of the Lord?
>> Or who has been his counselor?"
> "Who has ever given to God,
>> that God should repay them?"
> For from him and through him and for him are all things.
>> To him be the glory forever! Amen.

The apostle has taken us to theological grammar school. He is not shutting down all questions, doubts, conversations, or debates. As we read the rest of his New Testament letters, we will see that Paul happily engages in many of these sorts of conversations. But sometimes—just sometimes—the answer to our questions, the solution to our problems, will appear as a deeply offensive mystery that requires us to have faith, submitting to the authority and the truthfulness of God's revelation—whether or not its message coheres with our inherent human sense of justice or fair play. God alone is the Holy One, the Wholly Other, the one from whom we are separated by an Infinite Qualitative Difference.

Holiness and Holy War

What does Paul's explanation of the sovereignty of God's mercy in Romans 9 have to do with God's holiness? The connection is forged through the theme of offensiveness, more specifically the egregious offense caused by Old Testament accounts of divinely endorsed warfare. Old Testament stories of war are sometimes described as Holy War or Yahweh War. As the Israelites completed their wilderness wanderings and prepared to enter the land of Canaan, the land promised to them by Yahweh, they would continue to face significant obstacles. Most importantly, the land was not

Hidden Holiness

empty. This territory "overflowing with milk and honey" (Exod 3:8, 17; 13:5) was already occupied by the Canaanites: men, women, parents, grandparents, grandchildren, infants, brothers and sisters, families who loved each other as much as Israelite families loved each other.

Yahweh commanded his people to clear the land of Canaan, preparing it for Israel's imminent occupation, by *slaughtering the Canaanites* (Deut 7:1–2). The old occupants must be eradicated. Under Joshua's leadership,[1] Israel was told to begin a campaign to eliminate the inhabitants of the land (Deut 20:16–17; Josh 6:21, 24). Some would call it genocide.[2]

The climax of Israel's project required the complete destruction of all the people, livestock, and personal belongings from any city they conquered. Nothing could be kept as the personal spoils of war. Recall Achan's violent destruction for violating this rule after the conquest of Jericho (Josh 7:15–26). Everything was to be destroyed by fire as a sacrifice to Yahweh. This horrific act of worship was called "the ban," an English translation of the Hebrew word *ḥērem*.[3] This word forges a grammatical link connecting God's personal holiness with acts of *holy war. Ḥērem* means "to consecrate through destruction."[4] By denoting acts of sacrifice and consecration to God, however horrific they may have been, *ḥērem* shares the same semantic field[5] as the word *qadosh*, holy. Consequently, it is the most blood-curdling, shocking aspects of Israelite warfare that qualify Israel's conquest of Canaan as *holy war*.[6]

---

1. Joshua was the second-generation leader appointed by God to replace Moses.

2. For example, see Earl, *Joshua Delusion?*; Copan and Flannagan, *Did God Really Command Genocide?*; Gundry, ed., *Four Views on God and Canaanite Genocide*; Tinker, *Mass Destruction*; Trimm, *Destruction of the Canaanites*.

3. Some scholars refer to this holy war or Yahweh war as ḥērem warfare.

4. Or possibly "to destroy through consecration"; see Stern, *Biblical Herem*, 1, 40.

5. A semantic field is a collection of items referred to by a set of related words.

6. Holy war was commanded only against the Canaanites. Whether or not Yahweh fought alone, miraculously on Israel's behalf or used the Israelites to

The Problem with "the Problem" of Divine Violence

Naturally, many have objected to this Old Testament depiction of God, the same God who is described in the New Testament as the loving heavenly Father of Jesus of Nazareth. The apparent contrast between a wrathful Old Testament God of war and a loving New Testament God of grace led many in the early church to insist that these were two different Gods. The second-century church leader named Marcion, who was excommunicated as a heretic in 144 AD, taught that Israel's God was the wrathful, warrior Creator, while the Father of Jesus Christ was the savior God full of love and mercy. On this basis, Marcion simply cut the Old Testament out of the Christian Bible. According to him, the sacrificial death of Jesus on the cross has as much to do with a God of *holy war* as light has with darkness. For Marcion, the sacrificial life and ministry of Jesus becomes the only legitimate lens allowing us to see the loving character of the one true God. Marcion in those early days is not the only one seeking to distance God from these Old Testament narratives. In the words of theologian-pastor Gregory Boyd, "Jesus Christ crucified is the full and complete revelation of God. From him we learn that God's nature is love . . . Everything we need to know and can know about God is found in Christ."[7] In other words, the warrior God of the Old Testament can no longer be seen as a truthful representation of God's nature.

For such readers of the Old Testament, it seems obvious that the Father of the crucified Christ would never impose the horrors of *ḥerem* on anyone. Biblical scholar Gerd Lüdemann, writing two decades before Boyd, wrote similarly, "There is hardly anything in the Old Testament which provokes the abhorrence of the modern observer so much as the practice of the ban as the conclusion of a 'Holy War.'"[8] Repeatedly we are warned by many writers and scholars that this is a major problem demanding a solution. We are told that the viability of the church's gospel witness depends

---

fight with him is debated; see Lind, *Yahweh Is a Warrior*.

7. Boyd, *Cross Vision*, xi, 22. Boyd does not advocate the Old Testament's removal from the Christian canon, as did Marcion.

8. Lüdemann, *Unholy in Holy Scripture*, 37. Similar quotes from additional sources could be repeated many times over.

upon it. Yahweh's Old Testament violence must somehow be accounted for in a way that satisfies and comports with our own sense of goodness and justice and our contemporary evaluation of Jesus Christ as the savior who emphasized God's love. The title of Lüdemann's book, *The Unholy in Holy Scripture: The Dark Side of the Bible*, gives us a heads-up as to what his final conclusions will be in resolving the repugnant dilemma of Old Testament violence. According to Lüdemann, divine violence, that is *the unholy*, must be eliminated.

What is to be said in response to such well-meaning, heartfelt objections? Can a bloodthirsty warrior God be rehabilitated as the gracious Father of the crucified messiah? Can Yahweh remain holy after his red-handed involvement with unholy holy war?

Allowing God to Be God

There is a vast literature discussing this subject, and space prohibits a thorough examination of its complexities here. As I have done so far, I will continue foregrounding the matter of God's holiness and keeping it center stage. I will briefly touch on only a few of the more germane factors that I believe are important for properly answering these questions about the problem of divine violence.

It needs to be pointed out how remarkable it is to read through this body of literature that finds *holy war* language abhorrent and discover almost no accounting of what it means for the God of the Bible to be a holy God. It's a bit like editorializing on a recipe for crab salad without ever mentioning crab. In such discussions, God's holiness is the elephant in the room that nobody talks about. In fact, great energy is expended in evading the idea of divine holiness.

One exception to this assessment is Lüdemann's book, *The Unholy in Holy Scripture*. Yet, even Lüdemann proves disappointing in that he still has nothing to say about the biblical meaning of holiness. Instead, he remains content simply to repeat the standard ethical condemnations, saying such things as "cruelty remains cruelty even if it is ordained by God."[9]

The problems in dodging the question of God's holiness are paramount and cripple any attempt to construct a biblical account. To begin with, in Lüdemann's reckoning holiness remains a strictly moral, ethical category. There is no conception of God's Wholly Otherness. The second problem follows directly. Imagining that human beings can stand toe to toe with the Wholly Other, subjecting the Holy One to the same moral valuations we attach to human behavior ("cruelty remains cruelty"), demonstrates a complete and utter failure to contend with the Infinite Qualitative Difference distinguishing human judgment from divine judgment.

Space prevents us from going into the original cosmologies of spiritual power and cosmic combat attached to the ancient holy war practice of *ḥērem*, but Philip D. Stern provides a summary helpful for our purposes when he writes in his book, *The Biblical Herem: A Window on Israel's Religious Experience*, "Subjective considerations of justice have no place here. When one tampered with the deity's projection of the sacral sphere on this earth—[as did Canaanite wickedness, desecrating the promised land with cosmic chaos]—one is subject to the penalty imposed by the elemental nature of God."[10] The elemental nature of God is his holiness, his Wholly Otherness. *Holy war* is cosmic reconstruction performed by Israel's dangerous Redeemer. If no one can see the Holy One and live, no one can transgress the Holy One's cosmic design and survive to flaunt their violations with impunity. The Creator will intervene, calling down judgment where necessary, in order to restore the originally intended ordering of the cosmos, a cosmos that includes God's sovereignty over the promised land and its inhabitants.

Secondly, despite the oft-repeated contrast between the Old Testament warrior God and the merciful God revealed in Christ's death at Calvary, this contrast is more imaginary than substantial. To say that "Jesus Christ crucified is the full and complete

---

9. Lüdemann, *Unholy in Holy Scripture*, 49.
10. Stern, *Biblical Herem*, 224.

revelation of God" is true *as long as* we acknowledge the fullness of divine actions on display in the crucifixion. Unfortunately, Boyd, Lüdemann, and their fellow travelers fail to contend with the fact that the crucifixion is a bloody, repulsive act of violence *ordained by God* (Acts 2:23; 3:18; 4:28). As the final sacrifice for sin, Jesus' death on the cross displays God's love in that Christ dies a substitutionary death, taking our well-deserved punishment upon himself. However, the cross also displays God's wrath unfurled against human rebellion, the punishment of death—a most macabre, gruesome, tortuous, protracted death—poured out on the man who knew no sin (Heb 4:15; 1 Pet 2:22) but became a sin offering for us (Rom 8:3). I frankly find this consistent oversight to be astonishing. Jesus' heavenly Father willed this violent act of salvific injustice.

More than this, the Synoptic Gospels all describe three hours of darkness, from noon until three in the afternoon, blanketing the entire land of Judah while Jesus hung from the cross (Matt 27:45; Mark 15:33; Luke 23:44–45). The three-hour reign of darkness is climaxed by Jesus' lament, "My God, my God, why have you forsaken me?" Old Testament *holy war* narratives are frequently accompanied by such heavenly signs as eclipses and ominous darkness. Signs in the heavens signify the arrival of "the Day of the Lord," the day of God's wrath, that is the climactic, final battle of holy war when divine judgment is poured out onto the earth.[11] These signs provide celestial evidence of (a) Yahweh's personal activity in the destruction of his enemies, and (b) the fact that God is setting straight the sinful misalignment of his cosmos. The fundamental truth that holy war texts illuminated was that Yahweh triumphs over the monsters of chaos (such as sin and Satan). These stories are about how God restores his originally intended order for creation properly arranged in submission to his will. I strongly suspect that we are intended to understand Jesus' sacrificial death

11. See Isaiah 8:22; Jeremiah 15:9; Joel 2:2, 10, 30–31; 3:1–5, 15; Amos 8:9; Zephaniah 1:15; cf. Acts 2:17–21. Old Testament accounts of holy war often described Israel as Yahweh's disobedient enemy. Yahweh's execution of holy war was impartial. Yahweh fought against human rebellion, no matter where it came from, whether it was Canaanite or Israelite.

on the cross as *the final great battle of Yahweh's cosmic holy war, his day of wrath.*[12] Wrath offers us another view into divine holiness. At this moment, the powers of sin and death are finally defeated; they fall powerless into the dust at Jesus' feet, never to contest the Holy One's authority ever again.

So, when someone says "Jesus Christ crucified is the full and complete revelation of God" the question to ask is: "Is the divinely executed violence that we see at Calvary included within the full revelation of God?"[13] Is God's wrath, poured out upon the destructive power of sin, included within this complete revelation? If an account of God's action in Christ cannot account for the divine wrath over his enemies, we are simply being offered a sanitized but inadequate understanding of God, of holiness, of the cross, of sin, of Jesus' sacrifice, and of what it means to be counted among God's people.

Understanding Life in the New Covenant

Finally, some share the fear expressed by Charlie Trimm in his book *The Destruction of the Canaanites: God, Genocide, and Biblical Interpretation*. If Old Testament accounts of Yahweh's participation in holy war and *ḥērem* are not discredited or somehow delegitimized, then holy war is allowed to stand as a paradigm for modern nation-states to appropriate for their own malign purposes. Legitimizing interpretations of Old Testament holy war allows "for the possibility that God could call his people to do something similar today. This is not an implausible problem," Trimm warns, "as some in church history have claimed Joshua as precedent for their own violent actions."[14]

Of course, Trimm is right in warning about this danger. Western history is full of power-hungry actors eager to style themselves

---

12. For classic treatments of the place of divine wrath in the work of Christ, see Morris, *Apostolic Preaching of the Cross* and *Cross in the New Testament*.

13. To argue that these were human, not divine, actions is to evade the issue. They were foreordained by God. Doesn't that make God equally responsible?

14. Trimm, *Destruction of the Canaanites*, 91.

as the new Joshua preparing God's people to wage war against the modern Canaanites, whomever they may be. The solution to this ugly problem, however, is much simpler and more straightforward than scholars like Trimm recognize. The solution is *a better understanding of biblical theology*, not a wholesale reinterpreting of Old Testament warfare texts. The issue at stake concerns the nature of God's covenants and the transition from God's Sinai covenant with Israel to God's new covenant with Jesus Christ, Israel, and the rest of the world.

The Sinai covenant was forged between Yahweh and Israel at the foot of Mount Sinai. Israel's relationship with Yahweh was immediate and material. Obedience to the Lord's demands resulted in material blessings here and now (Deut 28:1–14). Disobedience brought physical, material punishment here and now (Deut 28:15–68). Remember Yahweh's warnings about the immediate destruction of anyone who transgressed the boundary lines draw at the foot of Mount Sinai (Exod 19:22, 24). The promised land of Canaan provided the earthly venue for Yahweh's material demonstrations of his faithfulness to Israel, both to bless and to punish. Conquering the land and eradicating wicked Canaanites were the physical, immediate manifestations of God's covenant promises working themselves out on Israel's behalf. Victory on the battlefield was evidence of Yahweh's blessing; defeat was a divine punishment.

But all of this changed with the advent of Jesus Christ. The new covenant, inaugurated through Jesus' suffering, death, and resurrection, transforms the Sinai covenant and replaces Yahweh's former methods of blessing and cursing his people materially in this life. The new covenant brings a new way of living by following the way of Jesus. Rewards and punishments are not doled out materially in this world. Instead, we look forward to the final judgment to hear God's verdict over our lives. Jesus will never ask his people to inflict violence, pain, or hardship—much less go to war—against anyone, including our most hostile enemies. The new covenant does not bind God to any particular chosen nation; there is no new covenant national equivalent of ancient Israel. God

The Problem with "the Problem" of Divine Violence

no longer uses armies to exact his revenge. Under the terms of the new covenant, the international, multiethnic collection of God's people are always to be peacemakers (Matt 5:9), people who love and pray for their enemies, who bless those who curse them (Matt 5:44–48). The LORD's new covenant people can have nothing to do with any forms of violence, bloodshed, or warfare.[15] Since the advent of Christ, God will never raise up another Joshua to lead his people into combat against anyone thought to be the new Canaanites of this world.

Confronting the Possibility of Offense

Of course, more could be said about how to deal with the challenges presented in the Old Testament accounts of *holy war*. We could discuss the historical reliability of the accounts; the strong possibility of hyperbole in the narratives of apparent genocide; and why it is that the very people who were supposedly wiped out on the battlefield often reappear later in the Old Testament narratives.[16] For some readers, no amount of nuance in our reading of the biblical texts can ameliorate the fact that the Old Testament contains stories where God commanded the wholesale elimination of the conquered, whether or not it happened as we might think at first reading. Even if complete *holy war* never occurred, the stories are repugnant in their own right. A disturbingly violent portrait of God is being depicted in holy Scripture! What good can come of that? Isn't indignation still the only proper response?

Genuine faith has always been confronted with such challenges. Every opportunity to believe in the mystery of the Holy One is simultaneously an opportunity to take offense at the things we cannot understand. Those scholarly attempts to erase the offensiveness of *holy war* and divine holiness are, in fact, efforts at

---

15. On the priority of nonviolence for God's people today, see my book *I Pledge Allegiance*, especially chapter 9, "Does Kingdom Service Permit Military Service?"

16. Copan and Flannagan, *Did God Really Command Genocide?*, 76–124, provide a good discussion of these interpretive issues.

erasing a genuine Christian faith, one that allows for mystery and for our finitude to be acknowledged. God fully comprehended is not God. And though this may seem like an attempt to evade an insuperable problem, I intend rather to humbly refer back to Paul's exclamation, "Who has known the mind of the Lord? Or who has been his counselor?" (Rom 11:34).

The possibility of offense is essential to grasping what it means for God to be Wholly Other. In the words of Kierkegaard:[17]

> But take away the possibility of offense, as has been done in Christendom . . . and then Christianity is abolished, has become something easy, a superficial something that neither wounds nor heals deeply enough; it has become the false invention of purely human compassion that forgets the infinite qualitative difference between God and man.

Discussion Questions:

1. The chapter begins its discussion of holy war by exploring Paul's argument in Romans 9–11. What parallels does the author draw between these two subjects? What light does Romans 9–11 shine onto finding an answer to "the problem" of Old Testament holy war?

2. How does Jesus' crucifixion relate to the Old Testament theme of holy war? What role does the cross have to play in showing that the God of the Old and New Testaments are the same God?

3. How does God's wrath relate to God's holiness?

4. The chapter claims that Christian faith will always be confronted by "the possibility of offense." Why is this the case? How have you faced the possibility of offense in your own Christian life? How have you worked through that challenge?

---

17. Kierkegaard, *Practice in Christianity*, 140.

Chapter Five

Holiness Becomes Relational

HAVING SHOWN THAT HOLINESS is about God's concern with God's self, we are now ready to examine the second dimension of God's holiness: specifically that God's holiness is relational. The supreme paradox of divine holiness, which we have outlined as God's otherness, is revealed in God's decision to enter into personal relationships with sinful people. The One who is Wholly Other chooses to stoop down for the sake of intimacy with fallen human beings along with the rest of creation. The Infinite Qualitative Difference separating the Holy One from humanity does not confine God to some cosmic throne room as if he were a heavenly hermit isolated from creation. The God who is Wholly Other does not wrap himself in a cocoon of impenetrable mystery, whispering like Greta Garbo, a major Hollywood star of a former era, "*I want to be alone.*"

Quite the opposite. The one who is absolutely unlike us is also the one who wants to build intimate personal relationship with us, so that we will know him as the Wholly Other who becomes wholly available to his people. God's love, shared with his creation, and his grace, demonstrated in his decision to make himself known, are additional aspects of God's holiness. For, as we will see as we look at the biblical narratives, it is as God revealed in his holiness, his holy otherness, that he bridges the gulf of infinite separation to bring us into relationship with himself and to make himself known through infinite love and graciousness.

Examining the stories of ancient Israel in the Bible, we discover this relational dimension of divine holiness. Freshly delivered from annihilation by Pharaoh's army at the Red Sea, the harried Israelites gathered at the foot of Mount Sinai to await Yahweh's instructions:

> You yourselves have seen what I did to Egypt, and how I carried you on eagles' wings and brought you to myself. Now if you obey me fully and keep my covenant, then out of all nations you will be my treasured possession. Although the whole earth is mine, you will be for me a kingdom of priests and a holy nation. (Exod 19:4–6)

Yahweh rescued Israel, brought them to himself, and chose them to become his holy nation. He first becomes Israel's Savior before becoming their Lawgiver. Becoming God's holy people is the realization of the earlier explanation given about the meaning of God's name, Yahweh, as "I will be with you" (Exod 3:12). God does not make Israel holy by somehow perfecting the nation such that they all act blamelessly. Far from it. It is his own divine presence, Yahweh's being "with them" in personal relationship that makes Israel a holy nation. God's nature is such that his holiness extends from him through the personal intimacy he brings in abiding with his people. The Holy One creates this new intimacy and promises to make Israel "a kingdom of priests and a holy nation" for as long as they commit to remaining in relationship with him. There is a required reciprocity in that they are obliged to obey the covenant God is establishing at Mount Sinai. However, their covenant obedience did not earn their status of "holy nation." The covenant is graciously established by Yahweh, who without obligation chose to deliver them from Egyptian bondage. Both Israel's deliverance and her status as "holy" are gifts of divine grace. The Holy One says, *I will share my holiness with you and make you a holy people for as long as you will remain in obedient relationship with me.* This is the significance of the if/then clause in Exodus 19:5. Yahweh's divine otherness embraces Israel, wrapped in his presence as in a radiant blanket. It is God who brings them to himself and wraps himself around them.

Holiness thus becomes relational, creating a new status for anyone who walks with God. This refrain is repeated often throughout Israel's story:

> I am the LORD who makes you holy (Exod 31:13).

> Keep my decrees and follow them. I am the LORD who makes you holy (Lev 20:8).

> The whole community is holy, every one of them, and the LORD is with them (Num. 16:3).

> For you are a people holy to the Lord your God. The Lord your God has chosen you out of all the peoples on the face of the earth to be his people, his treasured possession (Deut 7:6; also see 14:2, 21; 26:19; 28:9; Isa 4:3; Jer 13:11).

Holiness must be viewed relationally before it can be understood ethically. Holy living arises as the consequence of being embraced by the holy One who makes us holy by his living presence; it does not work the other way around.

The Contagion of Holiness

One curious aspect of God's relational holiness is that it is sometimes described in the Bible as being contagious. The description in Leviticus 6 of various sacrifices offers a dramatic example of this idea. In Leviticus 6:18 we are told that "whatever touches it [the grain offering] will become holy." Holiness is transferred through physical contact with the grain. Sin offerings in Leviticus are described as having the same effect. Leviticus 6:27 declares that "whoever touches any of the flesh [of the sacrificed animal] will become holy." We find similar language in Ezekiel where the prophet explains how the priests are to change their clothing before leaving the tabernacle's inner sanctum and going out to the outer court. They are to "put on other clothes, so that they do not consecrate the people by means of their garments" (44:19). Yahweh is present at the tabernacle and its altar; thus, God's presence makes holy these items and anyone who comes in contact with them. Any sacrifices and offerings brought to the altar become holy because the altar is holy. Thus, anyone who touches the sacrificial offerings becomes holy because the sacrifices were holy. Holiness can thus become a chain of sacred transformations like a holy chemical reaction. God's sanctity is always transformative, laying a positive claim to anything that God's holiness does not destroy.

Holiness and Sovereignty

Though God's holiness is intimate and relational, it remains his prerogative to impart. The Wholly Other Holy One can be known intimately, but he cannot be presumed upon nor controlled. The tragic events described in Numbers 16 illustrate the disastrous effects of being presumptuous in the light of God's holiness and ignoring the fearful danger of being unprepared to experience it. Korah and his followers complained to Moses about the need for greater equality of access to God among the people of Israel. They were not satisfied with merely being Levites and thus not being able to enter the holiest places in the tent of meeting. Korah reminded Moses of Yahweh's covenantal promise in Exodus 19:6, "The whole community is holy, every one of them, and the LORD is with them" (verse 3). On this basis he complained that others besides Moses and Aaron ought to be free to enter into the sacred space of Yahweh's holy presence, burn incense, offer sacrifices, and minister Yahweh's blessings to the people.

Moses ordered them all to gather together the next day, to burn incense in front of the tabernacle where the LORD would render his verdict on their claim. Would they be allowed to stand like priests in God's holy presence or not? Even as Moses warned the rest of the people to step away from Korah's company:

> . . . the ground under them split apart and the earth opened its mouth and swallowed them and their households, and all those associated with Korah, together with

Holiness Becomes Relational

> their possessions. They went down alive into the realm of the dead, with everything they owned; the earth closed over them, and they perished and were gone from the community. (Num 16:31–33)

Yahweh's holiness remained contagious. But for the disobedient, the kiss of holiness meant death. Even those specifically chosen to be God's holy people had to take care to respect God's holy presence. The obedient were blessed by their new status as holy ones. For the disobedient, however, like Korah and his company, Yahweh's holy embrace brought down fire and destruction from heaven (Num 16: 35–39).

Holiness and the Church

Given what we've seen as to the continuity of the Bible's teaching around the theme of God's holiness, these Old Testament emphases on the relational nature of holiness continue to be an emphasis into the new covenant. Continuity between Israel and the church is made explicit in 1 Peter 2:9 where Peter quotes from Exodus 19:5–6:

> Now if you obey me fully and keep my covenant, then out of all nations you will be my treasured possession. Although the whole earth is mine, you will be for me a kingdom of priests and a holy nation.

The original promises of relational holiness made to Israel at Mount Sinai are now fulfilled in those who surrender themselves to the lordship of Christ, demonstrating that they "have been chosen . . . through the sanctifying work of the Spirit, for obedience to Jesus Christ" (1 Peter 1:2). The international, multiethnic church now becomes a holy nation unto itself redefining human relationships around the person of Jesus Christ. The New Testament church is repeatedly referred to as an assembly of *saints*, which is simply an alternative English translation of the Greek word meaning *holy ones*.[1] Yahweh now draws near and shares his holiness with

---

1. See Rom 1:7; 8:27; 12:13, 15:25, 26, 27, 31; 16:2; 1 Cor 1:2; 6:1, 2; 14:33;

all those, whoever and wherever they may be, who follow and obey his one and only Son, the resurrected Jesus. Through membership in the new covenant, the international body of Christ becomes the new holy nation.[2]

How does this international body of believers in Jesus demonstrate that they have become the chosen people of God? According to David Peterson, author of the book *Possessed by God: A New Testament Theology of Sanctification and Holiness*, the New Testament language of sanctification—that is, to become holy, to be made holy—most often refers to a condition described as "positional sanctification."[3] Peterson argues that this is a "permanent status" or a "dedicated state" bestowed upon every Christian through faith in Christ (Rom 15:16).[4] He surmises: "Paul primarily uses the verb 'to sanctify' with reference to Christian conversion and incorporation into the community of believers (Rom 15:16; 1 Cor 1:2; 6:11; Eph 5:26)."[5] Although there are instances where sanctification is depicted as an ongoing, developmental process,[6] in most instances, when Paul uses this language, he portrays Christian sanctification as another way of describing the church as a gathering of "holy people." Paul's words in 1 Corinthians 1:2 are characteristic:

> To the church of God in Corinth, to those sanctified in Christ Jesus and called to be his holy people, together with all those everywhere who call on the name of our Lord Jesus Christ.

Notice that, on Peterson's reading, the believer's sanctification occurs the moment she begins to follow Jesus. Thus, God's

---

16:1, 15; 2 Cor 1:1; 8:4; 9:1, 12; 13:12; Eph 1:1; 4:12; Phil 1:1; Col 1:2; Acts 9:13, 32, 41.

2. See my detailed discussion of 1 Peter 2 and its implications in *Like Birds in a Cage*, 112–19.

3. Peterson, *Possessed by God*, 47.

4. Peterson, *Possessed by God*, 59, 142.

5. Peterson, *Possessed by God*, 67.

6. See especially Peterson, *Possessed by God*, chapter 4, "Pursuing Holiness," 69–92.

holy people are fully sanctified in Christ because Yahweh embraces them as his children when they call on the name of Jesus. God the Father imparts his holiness to all those who believe. God fills them with his Holy Spirit, and gathers them together in a new, Spirit-filled community called the body of Christ, the new assembly of God's holy people, his sanctified, treasured possession.

Furthermore, holiness also remains contagious in the New Testament. We already saw in chapter 3 how even Christians may suffer and die when God's holy wrath is expressed in those cases where believers dared to approach the Lord's holy presence inappropriately or presumptively. God's contagious holiness is also described in more positive terms in 1 Corinthians 7:14, where Paul commands married believers not to initiate divorce proceedings against an unbelieving spouse if the unbeliever is happy to remain married. Paul says:

> For the unbelieving husband has been sanctified through his wife, and the unbelieving wife has been sanctified through her believing husband. Otherwise, your children would be unclean, but as it is, they are holy.

According to the rest of Paul's theology, this does not mean that the unbelieving marriage partner and the couple's children are automatically redeemed in Christ. For this, they too must exercise faith. But the Holy Spirit who comes from the all-holy God lives within the Christian family member. Thus, other members of the household, including the unbelieving spouse, also dwell in God's holy presence. Thus, Paul declares that they are holy as well. In other words, they are unwittingly blessed by a closer proximity to God's saving grace than are those who have no personal, familial relationship with Christians at all.

Practical Response

To be chosen, loved, wanted, and rescued by the infinite, mysterious, all-powerful, personal God of holiness and wonder is, without doubt, the most beautiful, mind-boggling truth that any believer will ever know. What is an appropriate response to this incomprehensible, yet thrilling reality, this gift from our savior God?

First, *we should cultivate the habit of living before the Holy One with an attitude of awe and thanksgiving.* Think of it. The One who is unlike us in every essential way decided to leap across the Infinite Qualitative Difference in order to introduce himself, save us from our sins, and live with you and me in a gracious personal relationship of love, forgiveness, hope, and promise. The unfathomable Master Creator, the One who can string all the brilliant stars of the Milky Way onto an infinite strand of angelic thread, wants to bestow the priceless gift of unending grace upon your head, claiming you as his own.

As the blessed receivers of this unfathomable gift what else can we be but dumbfounded and filled with overflowing awe and thanksgiving? What else can we do but be brought to our knees and exalt our Holy Redeemer with unending praise and adoration? These words of wisdom from Karl Barth speak ever so urgently to us today:[7]

> A person to whom zeal for God's honor is alien can be no real Christian. And the one who has lost it can no longer be a Christian . . . We say categorically that from this standpoint there has to be in the Christian life a kind of necessary Christian passion: zeal for the honor of God.

As we discussed in chapter 1, this is embedded as a priority in praying the very first petition of the Lord's Prayer, beseeching the Holy One to exalt himself in the world. Those Christians who have never been discipled in such a way as to grasp something of the holiness of God will in turn be hard pressed to grasp Barth's sense of urgency. In that sense I disagree with Barth's black or white pronouncement. But believers of any age should all be nurtured in churches rooted in the Scriptures, where everyone is helped to grow in the knowledge that the Holy One is a God who deserves worship and to be exalted.

---

7. Barth, *Christian Life*, 115.

Holiness Becomes Relational

One useful and specific discipline for cultivating such zeal is the practice of praying through the book of Psalms. Find a psalm that extols God's holiness and the greatness of his character, sit with it, read it over and over again, meditate on it, imagine it, pray through it line by line, word for word, making its words your own exclamations of zealous wonder. For example, try it now with this portion of Psalm 97:

> 1 The LORD reigns, let the earth be glad;
>   let the distant shores rejoice.
> 2 Clouds and thick darkness surround him;
>   righteousness and justice are the foundation of his throne.
> 3 Fire goes before him
>   and consumes his foes on every side.
> 4 His lightning lights up the world;
>   the earth sees and trembles.
> 5 The mountains melt like wax before the Lord,
>   before the LORD of all the earth.
> 6 The heavens proclaim his righteousness,
>   and all peoples see his glory.

Immerse yourself in those words. Let them inundate you with the rising tide of God's glory. Let them penetrate your imagination until thoughts about the Holy One are the most beautiful thoughts you can ever think. They describe the holy heavenly Father who proved his infinite, immeasurable, blazing holy love for you by sending his one and only Son to die on a cross. Adore him. Thank him. Commit yourself to serving him for the rest of your life. Ask him to show you more and more of who he is and who he wants to become for you in your life.

Second, *focus on what the Holy Redeemer has already done for you*. The Father has made you one of his holy people, to thrive as a member of his holy assembly, his church. We all struggle with temptation and sin and, at times, we fall into disobedience and grieve the Holy Spirit by fresh betrayals of our calling as God's holy people. When that happens, the last thing we should do is wallow in our shame. Guilt and shame have no purchase on God's holy people. Rather, we need to turn around, repent of our sin as we confess our guilt to the Holy One. As we make whatever amends may be necessary, we must remind ourselves, "*I am one of God's saints!*" Tell yourself, "Jesus Christ has already sanctified me. I am made whole by the One who is Wholly Other. My Father sees no guilt in me. I am perfectly sinless in my savior, Jesus Christ." And then commit yourself again, and again, and again, and as often as is necessary, to be what you are.

The Father has already made you a holy person through the work of Jesus Christ and the indwelling of his Holy Spirit. So be what you are. Live a holy life because you are already a holy person. You are already a saint before God. Your relationship with the Holy One precedes your thoughts and behaviors. So, determine that your thoughts and behaviors will conform to your standing before the Holy One. You are, right now, already the holiest of companions to the Holy One. Yes, it is amazing and mind-boggling, but despite our reluctance to accept this unbelievable truth, it is true.

Third, *focus attention on the God you love rather than the sins you hate*. The best way to successfully conclude a long-distance journey is to look ahead and focus on the final destination. Looking backwards with too much attention on the journey's starting point is an excellent way to get lost and discouraged. Holy people, yes, even you and I, focus on where they are going, and where they are going is into the arms of their holy God. The Father's love draws us to himself. Being drawn closer to the Holy One will pull us away from sin and failure. This does not mean that we ignore our moral failures or sweep our sins under the rug. Practical and pastoral wisdom tell us that sin and guilt require confession and repentance. But then we remember that the Greek word for repentance means "turning around," and in turning away from sin we turn ourselves back towards the face of God, the God who loves us. Maintaining that Godward focus remains the best antidote to relapsing into waywardness. As we grow and become strengthened in our devotion to our heavenly Father, rebelling against him becomes less and less feasible. Sadly, the opposite is also true. The longer I stare at my sin—even once having confessed my guilt and received Christ's forgiveness—the more likely I will behave like that proverbial, hapless dog that eventually "returns to its vomit" (Prov 26:11). How much better to focus on God's perpetual call to feast together at his banqueting table in sanctity and devotion.

Fourth, *participate regularly in the holy assembly of God's holy people*. Remember that holiness is contagious. When Christians gather together to adore their savior, to extoll the Father's majesty, to become awestruck by his power and grace, to thank him for his immeasurable gifts, and to share the Holy Spirit's promptings with each other, we are burnishing the personal holiness that Christ has given to each of us. We rub off onto each other, helping one another to remain on the straight and narrow path to the kingdom of God. Our collective holiness always shines a bit more brightly after we worship and share our faith together. Collective adoration penetrates to the core of Christian identity and can serve our spiritual renewal. We may enter community gatherings disheartened and disheveled. But we can leave as sparkling saints, renewed, refreshed, and reminded that the Wholly Other has transformed us and remade us into his own treasured possession.

Fifth, *give yourself to those who are struggling*. For many believers, Christian gatherings can be more depressing than helpful, if they can even force themselves to darken the church door. I recently heard from a friend who told me that he couldn't bring himself to attend church anymore because everyone appeared to be so *perfect*. His life was falling apart, but he could not believe that any of the people he saw at church could possible identify, much less empathize, with his situation. He feared that if they knew his story, he would be shunned. He felt absolutely alone, and if anything, church made him feel even more lonely. The last thing in the world he could ever hope to become was a holy person.

This is the human condition for both saints and sinners, but especially for saints who recognize that they remain sinners. We must remember that we have been *made* holy. No one but God is *inherently* holy. We may never claim our sanctification as our own accomplishment. Thus, we maintain both the freedom and the obligation to confess our sins to each other. The Christian

Hidden Holiness

church should be the last place on earth where anyone *is made* to feel inferior or unwelcome.[8] God's holy people should be the most transparent, empathetic, authentic, and welcoming group of people anyone could ever meet. Remember Paul's encouragement to the church at Rome:

> Share with the Lord's people who are in need. Practice hospitality. Bless those who persecute you; bless and do not curse. Rejoice with those who rejoice; mourn with those who mourn. Live in harmony with one another. Do not be proud, but be willing to associate with people of low position. Do not be conceited. Do not repay anyone evil for evil. Be careful to do what is right in the eyes of everyone. (Rom 12:13–17)

Authentic personal relationships are crucial for any community of holiness. As we confess our sins to each other we remember that there is little if any difference between us. We all stand in need of the same gifts of grace from our common Savior. So, we invite transparency by being transparent ourselves. We "rejoice with those who rejoice, and we mourn with those who mourn." And we count it a privilege "to carry each other's burdens" (Gal 6:2), no matter what they may be, by talking honestly together. Invite people to become honest with you by being honest with them. Then pray together. Help each other. Love each other. Meet each other's needs. And remind each other *to be what you already are*. You are already the Father's holy treasure. So, lift your head and live like God's holy treasure.

Being Human with a Friend

Some years ago, my family was enjoying our vacation together in northwest Montana. A close friend of my oldest daughter stopped in to visit us for a few days as he made a cross-country trip from Oregon to the Midwest. This young man had been raised in a

---

8. The feelings that we create within ourselves is one thing. The feelings that we impose upon others are altogether different.

Christian household. His parents brought all their children to a famous West Coast congregation. He had grown up listening to the sermons of one of America's most famous radio preachers. Yet, he had walked away from the Christian faith at a very young age. We had spoken several times about his religious beliefs, his thoughts on Christianity and Jesus Christ, and I had shared my own Christian story with him. Most recently, as we sat together in the cozy living room of our vacation cabin, he was describing his family life and upbringing. He eventually confessed that one of the reasons that Jesus held no appeal for him was because his family's brand of Christian faith never struck him as real or authentic. In fact, he told me that "it wasn't human." He was looking for a faith that would fit with his humanity, not turn him into a spiritual fraud with a perpetual plastic smile and another "thank you Jesus!" shouted over every heartache.

I understood what he was saying.

As we spoke, I received an international call from a dear Palestinian friend who lives in a West Bank refugee camp on the border of Israel. I quickly debated with myself over whether I should take the call in another room. You see, Israel was brutally bombarding the Gaza Strip and my friend was grieving for his people who were suffering this grotesque military assault. Israeli forces were also carrying out a fierce military incursion in the West Bank that was inflicting daily violence onto all the people who lived there. I know myself well enough to know that I would break down and cry at some point in the conversation. But I suddenly felt very self-conscious about this. I didn't want my guest to see me cry over the phone.

But why not? I settled my internal debate by deciding to have my phone conversation in the living room with my family and our friend. And, naturally, I cried. I cried as I listened to stories of suffering. I cried as we talked about the bombardment of Gaza. I cried as I told him I was praying for him, asking that Jesus would protect him and his family from any and all danger.

Finally, I hung up the phone and began to wipe away my tears. Yes, I was self-conscious, wondering what our guest would make of my lack of control.

Eventually, he looked at me and said, "That was human."

And we talked about why I cried. We discussed Jesus and the Israel-Palestinian conflict. The holy Spirit reminded me that only humans are made into holy people. And holy people cry. Holy people are genuine and transparent. Holy people invite others to share in their experience of holiness with Jesus. Holy people admit their brokenness. And then holy people always remind themselves and others who know the Father to be what they are: *holy human beings.*

Discussion Questions:

1. The apostle Paul says that every Christian is a saint, is already a holy person. If faith in Christ makes every believer a holy person here and now, how does this status interact with the moral necessity of becoming a holy person? Isn't this a contradiction?

2. The chapter describes five actions for Christians to take in confirming their status as holy people. Which one(s) speaks most powerfully to you right now? What can you do to implement this behavior in your life today?

3. The chapter concludes with an emphasis on our humanity, on being a holy *human being*. Why is this emphasis important? Have you ever struggled with this, either in your relationship with yourself or with someone else? Explain.

Chapter Six

Be Holy as I Am Holy

TELLING MYSELF TO BECOME *what I am*—that is, a holy person—reminds me that being one of God's people comes with responsibility. It is a privileged status paired with obligation. We must live holy lives. This is expressed repeatedly throughout Scripture, starting in the Old Testament book of Leviticus: "I am the LORD your God; consecrate yourselves and be holy, because I am holy" (Lev 11:44, also v. 45). "Consecrate yourselves and be holy, because I am the LORD your God. Keep my decrees and follow them. I am the LORD who makes you holy" (Lev 20:7–8).[1]

There are three closely interrelated ideas in these verses. First, the Holy One has brought me into relationship with himself and made me holy; this is my permanent, irrevocable status as a child of God (see the discussion in the previous chapter). Second, being holy requires that I live a holy life; this responsibility is a permanent call on my life as a child of God. Finally, God is the Holy One who makes me holy and provides for me the holy standard that I may continue living in holiness.

Remembering that our God is Wholly Other sets an impossibly high bar. We can never become as God who remains alone, Wholly Other by an Infinite Qualitative Difference. We remain thus very much unlike God. Many centuries ago, the early church

---

1. Also see Lev 19:2; 20:26; 21:8; 22:31–33.

condemned as heresy (if not blasphemy) any notion that we can access some hidden spark of divinity tucked away within our corrupted humanity. We need to remember that we will always stand on the creaturely side of creation, distinct from our Creator. Yet, at the same time the call to be holy must also set us apart from the rest of creation. It should "other" us. We cannot be Wholly Other, but we ought to distinguish ourselves from the corruption of this fallen world. We cannot become God, but we can become godly. We are called to separate ourselves from wickedness, even as we face the challenge of entering into the messiness of human relationships. Just as the Holy One entered this sinful world in order to redeem it, we too must participate robustly in this world's messiness while simultaneously refusing to be corrupted by or conformed to our fallen age.

In the Old Testament, the standards for holy obedience were set by the terms of the Sinai covenant. The covenant established general ethical requirements for devotion, justice and mercy—to love God and your neighbor—required of everyone. The covenant also established specific demands for cleanliness and ritual purity, applied variously to priests, Levites and the general population. Hence, we read the Levitical call "*to consecrate* yourselves and be holy" (Lev 11:44; 20:7). To be consecrated means to be set apart for God's use. To be obedient to Yahweh, every Israelite was instructed to follow a number of purity regulations governing such things as food preparation, how to clean a house, wearing proper clothing, purifying the body, planting a field, plowing a field, to list only a few. All of these regulated activities contributed to the individual's, and the nation's, consecration—that is, its ability to be of service to God

To many modern readers, this complicated legal and ritual dimension of the Sinai covenant seems to be little more than an oppressive burden of a primitive religion or the whimsical rules of a controlling deity. But that was not the perspective of the Israelite people. For them, the covenant, with its accompanying laws and rules, was God's gift, instructing them in how best to please their Savior God in every situation. Whatever the circumstances, devout Israelites could ask themselves: What does the Lord ask of me in this situation? Has Yahweh given me instructions about how I should perform these tasks?

If we set our Christian, Protestant, anti-law prejudices aside and stop to reflect for a moment, that is not a bad mindset to cultivate. I would even say that it would be beneficial for every Christian to develop the habit of thinking this way: What is the Holy One asking of me in this, in every, situation? The New Testament makes clear that Christ, through his sacrifice at Calvary, inaugurates a new covenant, such that the demands of purification need not fall on us as Jesus fulfilled the law on our behalf. Still, the Old Covenant law testified to this new covenant and like the ancient Israelites, we too ought to orient ourselves towards pleasing the Lord and loving our neighbor by keeping what Jesus calls the two greatest commandments in Matthew 22: 37–40:

> "Love the Lord your God with all your heart and with all your soul and with all your mind." This is the first and greatest commandment. And the second is like it: "Love your neighbor as yourself." All the Law and the Prophets hang on these two commandments.

The dual nature of holiness, as both gift and obligation, including the importance of consecrating ourselves established in Leviticus, continues to be taught in the New Testament. We find that in 1 Peter 2:9 the Christian church (composed of believing gentiles *and* Jews) is referred to as a "holy nation," that is heirs to the promises of Exodus 19:5–6. As we saw in chapter 4, New Testament authors repeatedly refer to Christian communities as gatherings of *the saints,* those who are already sanctified and made into a holy people.[2]

The New Testament also calls us to grow in holiness, becoming holy even as we are already holy. 1 Peter 1:15–16 restates the complex of ideas examined above. Quoting Leviticus, the apostle Peter writes, "But just as he who called you is holy, so be holy in

---

2. Rom 1:7; 8:27; 12:13; 15:25, 26, 27, 31; 16:2; 1 Cor 1:2; 6:1, 2; 14:33; 16:1, 15; 2 Cor 1:1; 8:4; 9:1, 12; 13:12; Eph 1:1; 4:12; Phil 1:1; Col 1:2; Acts 9:13, 32, 41.

all you do; for it is written: 'Be holy, because I am holy.'"³ Again, just as our God is holy, so we must become holy in all we do. The goals, if not the means, of godly living remain consistent in both the Sinai and the new covenants, though now believers are filled with the Holy Spirit.

The New Testament makes it clear that holiness is a requirement to be received by God on judgment day. The author of Hebrews declares, "Make every effort to live in peace with all men and to be holy; without holiness no one will see God" (Heb 12:14). Similarly, 2 Peter 3:11 starkly underlines this warning, "Since everything will be destroyed in this way [by the fire of judgment], what kind of people ought you to be? You ought to live holy and godly lives as you look forward to the day of God and speed its coming." Living a holy life is essential in anticipating salvation at Christ's return. In fact, Peter says that the church's progress in holiness is somehow instrumental in "speeding its coming." Might we consider that Christ's return is actually held back by the slovenly hand of a lackadaisical church riddled with sin and worldliness? The apostle Paul agrees with Peter, warning the Galatian church that those who continue to "indulge the sinful nature" (Gal 5:19), by persistently engaging in the kinds of sins listed in verses 19–21, "will not inherit the kingdom of God" (verse 21). These passages suggest that at the end, what God desires most for his people is that they continue joyfully maturing in godly obedience, conforming more and more fully to the image of his one and only Son, preparing ourselves to meet him face to face.

Keeping In Step with the Spirit

As far as the New Testament is concerned, the ability to grow in holiness begins with faith in Christ and the presence of the Holy Spirit in a person's life. No passage makes this point more clearly than Galatians 5:13–26.⁴ Paul begins his discussion of Christian

---

3. See Lev 11:44, 45; 19:2; 20:7.

4. Of course, Galatians 5 is not the only New Testament passage dealing with the process of becoming holy. For similar theology and practical advice,

love (verse 13-14) by reminding the Galatian church about the Old Testament roots of the Spirit's love command. Quoting from Leviticus 19:18, the command to "love your neighbor as yourself" becomes the thesis statement for all that follows because it summarizes the whole of God's moral concern. "The entire law is summed up in this one command," Paul says (verse 14a). Personal holiness is profoundly relational just as divine holiness is relational (see chapter 5). Paul encourages the development of holy relationships with our neighbors that radiate with acts of loving kindness.

Living consistently with divine love as the hallmark of personal relationships arises from the internal, empowering work of the Holy Spirit. Christians are indwelt by the Spirit *of holiness*, who is busily at work empowering us to become holy even as we receive divine holiness as a gift. Paul repeats the centrality of the Spirit's role three times in this passage: "So I say, live by the Spirit, and you will not gratify the desires of the sinful nature" (verse 16). "If you are led by the Spirit, you are not under law" (verse 18). "Since we live by the Spirit, let us keep in step with the Spirit" (verse 25). Living by, being led by, keeping in step with the Holy Spirit are expressions of the Spirit's rich and complex work in our lives. First, Paul's Spirit admonitions are about resting confidently in the finished work of Jesus Christ, through whom we receive the Holy Spirit in the first place. As another New Testament author puts it, we should be: "Keeping our eyes on Jesus, the author and perfecter of our faith." (Heb 12:2) This will fasten us securely to the bedrock of the Christian life: God's promise that we are *already* sanctified as God's holy people.

Second, Paul's admonition to keep in step with the Spirit means that we are listening for the Spirit's direction and responding to the Spirit's promptings. Paul explains that every believer's life is the scene of a spiritual battle between "the sinful nature" (verses 16, 17, 19, 24) and the Holy Spirit. We regularly are faced with two competing spiritual urges:

---

see Rom 12:1-29; 2 Cor 3:2-18; Col 3:1-17; Eph 4:22—5:21; 1 Thess 4:1-10; 2 Tim 2:14-26; Titus 1:7-16; Jas 4:1-12; 1 Pet 1:13-2:3; 4:1-19.

> So I say, walk by the Spirit, and you will not gratify the desires of the flesh. For the flesh desires what is contrary to the Spirit, and the Spirit what is contrary to the flesh. They are in conflict with each other, so that you do not do what you want. (verses 16–17; also see Rom 7:15–20)

The Holy Spirit and the sinful nature—that is, the inclination to disobey God and go our own way—are in continual competition within us. Our sinful nature makes us susceptible to temptation, but it can never control us because Christ vanquished it once and for all on the cross. We become dead to sin and "slaves to righteousness"—that is, faithfulness and obedience to God—through Jesus' death, burial, and resurrection (Rom 6:17–23). Paul assures us, "Those who belong to Christ Jesus have crucified the sinful nature with its passions and desires" (verse 24). Here we confront another paradox of the Christian life. On the one hand, for as long as I remain in this fallen world, I will never be free of the problems of sin and temptation. Conversely, in any given moment, I am never obligated to indulge sin. The "passions and desires of the sinful nature" can no longer control me since their power to do so were broken in the crucifixion of Jesus. I am always free to act in the power of the Spirit, saying "no" to temptation and "yes" to obedience. Whenever that happens, I have demonstrated that I am "keeping in step with the Spirit."

Third, Paul's Spirit admonition suggests that making the moral choices consistent with life in the Spirit is not an entirely subjective affair. It never simply boils down to *how I feel* about a situation.[5] The Lord has given us a great deal of instruction to help us learn to hear the Spirit's voice. Paul begins by offering a list of behaviors and attitudes which are the fruit of the sinful nature (Gal 5:19–21). We can always be certain that the Holy Spirit will *never* lead us down such pathways. This representational list of sinful behaviors and thoughts (from sexual immorality to hatred and jealousy) is a sort of barometer for our spiritual life. Walking such

---

5. Learning to distinguish between my personal feelings and the promptings of the Spirit is an aspect of wisdom and discernment acquired with godly experience.

paths reveals that somewhere along the way we stopped attending adequately to the Spirit. It's high time to confess, repent, and return to Jesus. Paul goes so far as to warn us that anyone persisting in such sinful misbehavior "will not inherit the kingdom of God" (Gal 5:21; Heb 12:14). In other words, the only way a person can ignore the Spirit's directions so consistently, so egregiously as to end up in a persistently sinful lifestyle—with no inclination to turn around and run back to Jesus like the prodigal son (Luke 15:11–32)—is to risk grieving the Spirit and finding ourselves estranged from God altogether. Paul is clear: *the sinful nature has been crucified for all those belonging to Christ* (Gal 5:24).

With our sinful natures crucified in Christ, and God's ongoing work through the Spirit's presence, we can have confidence in God's working out holiness in our lives as his children. The presence of the Holy Spirit will always produce some fruit for righteousness (Gal 5:22–26). Certainly, we see the process of that fruit working itself out at different paces with different people. For all of us, our responsibility is to cultivate that fruit, so that it can grow and expand until it fills our lives completely, leaving no room for disobedience or rebellion. We will approach every situation, and every relationship, as another opportunity to display the fruit of the Spirit—love, joy, peace, patience, kindness, goodness, faithfulness, gentleness, and self-control (verses 22–23).

Holiness and Suffering

So far, our study of holy living has focused on the New Testament letters. From there we now examine *the role of suffering* in the development of a holy life. For Christians, our model in our pursuit of holiness is, and always will be, Jesus of Nazareth. That's why we must pay particular attention to his ethical instructions if we are to grow in obedience as we live in the kingdom of God. As I argued in my book *I Pledge Allegiance: A Believer's Guide to Kingdom Citizenship in 21st-Century America,* which focuses on the radical nature of Jesus' kingdom ethic, "God's kingdom brings a clear reversal of values for all its citizens, thoroughly subverting the commonly accepted norms of polite society. In fact, Jesus makes adherence to this reversal axiomatic for his followers."[6] This ethic-of-reversal runs as a bright red thread all throughout Jesus' teaching. It is encapsulated in Jesus' aphorism, "Whoever tries to keep his life will lose it, and whoever loses his life will preserve it" (Luke 17:33)—a most contrarian ethic if there ever was one. Losing one's life, pursuing a lifestyle of self-denial and sacrifice, is the only avenue to gaining eternal life with God. Significantly, Luke 17 places this saying in the middle of a lengthy explanation describing the final revelation of the kingdom of God on judgment day (Luke 17:20–37). Losing one's life for the kingdom is the only acceptable "exercise regimen" that can get a follower of Jesus "in shape" for an eternal future with the Holy One.

The entire pattern of Christ's life makes this point clear. Jesus had to suffer, face human temptation, and endure an excruciating death *before* he was able to ascend into the glory of his Father's company. In the New Testament, the normal pattern of the Christian life is that suffering precedes glory. Hebrews 2:10, 18 tell us, "In bringing many sons and daughters to glory, it was fitting that God, for whom and through whom everything exists, should make the pioneer of their salvation perfect through what he suffered . . . Because he himself suffered when he was tempted, he is able to help those who are being tempted." Similarly, Romans 8:17 encourages believers to remember, "Now if we are children, then we are heirs—heirs of God and co-heirs with Christ, if indeed we share in his sufferings in order that we may also share in his glory."

Sharing in Jesus' sufferings is (a) normative for every Jesus–follower, and (b) the expected prelude to sharing in the Father's eternal glory. Here *glory* refers to the public exhibition of holiness; *glory is holiness on display*. Thus, we will finally share in God's glory as the glory of our own personal holiness is united with the eternal glory of the Holy One. Then all things will be made public, including the Spirit's role in transforming us into an obedient, holy people. Through this God will be glorified as our holiness is revealed. There is, as usual in the matters of God's glory and holiness,

---

6. Crump, *I Pledge Allegiance*, 33.

a serious and frightening side. The apostle Paul also writes in another epistle that on judgment day the righteous will be separated from the wicked (who go to "everlasting destruction" absent the Lord's presence). Even and maybe because of this real danger, it is all the more astounding as good news that the Lord "comes *to be glorified in his holy people* and to be marveled at among all those who have believed" (2 Thess 1:10). The Lord will glorify himself *in us* as his holiness in publicly displayed through our ultimate perfection. And we will marvel at the final results of a sanctification process that we never fully understood until that moment even as we see what this process has saved us from.

Returning to Romans 8:17, the conditional nature of Paul's promise should not be overlooked: We are co-heirs with Christ *if* we are children, and *if* we share in his sufferings. The lives of God's children are marked by struggles, sacrifice, pain, and opposition. Sometimes this opposition is targeted against us because we follow Jesus. But at other times, our struggles are simply the result of living in a broken world that no longer functions as the Creator originally intended. In any event, suffering as Jesus suffered is primary evidence that we are in step with the Holy Spirit, following hard after Jesus, maturing in personal holiness, and on track to be received by God on the day of Christ's return.

The inverse implication should not be missed. If living a Christian life *never* creates difficulties for us; never leaves us the odd one out; never pushes us to live contrary to society's expectations, then we ought to consider if we are indeed on a path of holiness before God. Likewise, the apostle Peter warns us, "If you suffer as a Christian, do not be ashamed, but praise God that you bear that name. For it is time for judgment to begin with God's household" (1 Pet 4:16b–17). Godly suffering is one of the means God uses to purify the church of Christ. Thus, judgment begins with believers. This will reveal who welcomes suffering in solidarity with Jesus and who evades that suffering through accommodation or faithlessness. In short, our judgment will reveal if we are on the path of holiness or teetering on the edge of perdition.

Hidden Holiness

Of course, when we think of the sufferings of Jesus, initially we conjure images of Calvary, including his arrest, mockery, beatings, brutal crucifixion, and lingering death. Sometimes, like Jesus, believers face death as the ultimate cost of discipleship. Although threats of Christian martyrdom are not likely in the United States today, there are many places in the world where faithfulness to Jesus Christ can still be a life-or-death affair. The temptation to compromise our faithfulness to Christ, or to renounce him altogether, in exchange for saving our lives is not a situation I would wish on anyone. Yet, many believers around the world are regularly called to prove their holiness by resisting temptation to the bitter end and dying for Christ their Savior.[7]

Few, if any, of us will ever face violent martyrdom as an expression of our faithfulness. But we all are called to persevere through a wide range of everyday suffering that challenges all believers everywhere. Not all of these everyday struggles are elicited by our sinful nature. Sometimes they are the mundane results of life in a fallen world. We *groan* with the rest of a fallen universe (Rom 8:18–27) as we live in a world that no longer works as originally intended. Painful afflictions, sickness, and death are each opportunities to cultivate the fruit of the Spirit even though they are rarely due to personal sinfulness. Regardless of the cause of our suffering, the New Testament offers profound and clear encouragement. Christ's passion was only the climax to a lifetime of suffering. Being "made like us in every way" (Heb 2:17), Jesus understands the full measure of suffering that our regular, daily temptation can provoke in us. Like us, Jesus "suffered when he was tempted" (Heb 2:18). And he was "tempted in every way, just as we are" (Heb 4:15). Being tempted like us in every way, Jesus experienced the struggles and difficulties that can arise when we say "no" to temptation. As Jesus was tempted like us in every way, his life was marked by similar daily temptations and other forms of daily suffering such as is common to all of us.

---

7. For contemporary examples of such persecution around the world, see Shortt, *Christianophobia*.

Our experience of suffering through temptation, when compared to the life of Jesus, is far more limited and finite. The gap separating our experience of temptation from Jesus' experience of temptation reveals how much we are also *unlike* him. Uniquely and quite unlike us, Jesus never surrendered to temptation. We frequently cut short the temptation experience by yielding to it, by surrendering ourselves to sin. Jesus, on the other hand, never surrendered, enduring every temptation for as long as it persisted. Those who have matured in holiness may also have resisted for the duration. However, none of us resist completely, every time, or all the time. How much more strenuous must Jesus' resistance have been, wringing out the last drop of bitter testing every time it assaulted him.

Furthermore, we also confront temptation as fallen human beings, all too familiar with sin. Jesus faced temptation as the eternal, sinless Son of God. My point is not to diminish the reality of Jesus' temptations or to suggest that Christ's deity insulated him from either the gruesome weight of temptation or the possibility of sinning. Though divine, Jesus' full humanity confronted him with the possibility that he could fail a test or that he could surrender to temptation. In this regard, he was truly tempted as we are. Jesus knows what it means to stand at the precipice of surrendering to sin *just as we do*. The glorious difference is that he never surrendered.

The great contrast between our familiarity with sin and Jesus' complete unfamiliarity with falling into sin profoundly highlights *the greater degree of revulsion* that Jesus would have felt when he managed to resist each and every temptation to rebel against his heavenly Father. As such, Jesus faced a unique kind of suffering that none of us will ever understand. Jesus experienced a degree of suffering through temptation that goes far beyond anything we can imagine even in our darkest struggles. I suspect that we catch a glimpse of this degree of suffering when we see Jesus weeping in the garden of Gethsemane, pleading with God the Father for some way to accomplish God's purposes without facing death on the cross (Luke 22:41–44).

Of course, sometimes we *do* suffer like Jesus, resisting faithfully all the way through temptation. For many walking in holiness, over time, the degree of suffering diminishes throughout a lifetime with the formative power of ongoing spiritual victory. Forming the habit of saying "no" to particular sins eventually becomes the order of the day. In such a highly sexualized society as modern America, temptations towards illicit sex abound. Resisting these temptations, and eliminating the circumstances that foster temptation, requires significant self-discipline and a supreme commitment to conform our lives to Jesus' model, no matter the cost. Yet, I know people who have and are doing exactly this—by pursuing a Spirit-directed life in such a way that eventually sexual temptation becomes a nonissue.

The same could be said of such sins as greed and acquisitiveness, pride and self-promotion. These too are temptations contrary to the life of the Spirit but blatantly promoted in American society. Renouncing them requires heightened levels of self-awareness, self-control, and a dedication to self-renunciation and servanthood that will challenge the willpower of even the most dedicated disciple. But it is possible. Yes, the Spirit always empowers us, as we too must choose to say "no" to the flesh and "yes" to the Spirit. The apostle Peter expresses this dynamic quite dramatically when he writes, "Since Christ suffered in the body, arm yourselves also with the same attitude, because he who has suffered in the body is done with sin" (1 Pet 4:1). What kind of fool would willingly endure pain and hardship if it could easily be avoided by going with the flow, *unless* this person loved Jesus Christ more than they hated suffering? Those who willingly suffer now as faithful disciples demonstrate that they are turning their backs to the allure of sin.

Such suffering can express itself in many different ways. Not all suffering is physical. It can also be psychological, emotional, or situational. These experiences can be encountered in many life settings, such as alienation from family members; losing friends; giving up a favorite pastime; cutting ourselves off from unhealthy associations; abandoning long-cherished plans; risking life changes that scare us; being mocked or ridiculed; losing a promotion or a job. To willingly suffer here and now shows that we have said goodbye to disobedience and are walking the road of holiness leading to eternal glory.

Keeping Our Eyes on the Prize

The Scriptures offer substantial encouragement to persevere in keeping in step with the Holy Spirit regardless of the difficulties this causes us. Both the apostles Paul and Peter in their epistles remind us to keep our experiences in proper perspective. This life is temporary; its pain is short-lived. Even if the pain lasts our entire life, this life is but the blink of an eye compared to the beautiful expanse of eternity. Peter assures us that "the God of all grace, who called you to his eternal glory in Christ, *after you have suffered a little while*, will himself restore you and make you strong, firm and steadfast" (1 Pet 5:10). Similarly, Paul encourages the Corinthians to keep their eyes on heaven's prize, "for our *light and momentary troubles* are achieving for us an eternal glory that far outweighs them all. So, we fix our eyes not on what is seen, but on what is unseen, since *what is seen is temporary*, but what is unseen is eternal" (2 Cor 4:17–18).

Whatever suffering we may endure in this world, as we grow in holiness by keeping in step with the Spirit, is nothing compared to the glory we will share with the Holy One in eternity. God's glory will be revealed in us as our holiness is merged with his. This sounds like "pie in the sky by and by" only to those who have yet to experience the hope, power, and encouragement that comes from the Holy One when we suffer for his sake while fixing our eyes on the invisible promises of the kingdom of God.

Discussion Questions:

1. In what ways can the Levitical charge "to consecrate ourselves and be holy" serve as a directive for Christians today?

2. The chapter argues that followers of Jesus "become holy" by "keeping in step with the Spirit." Explain what this means. How have you grown over the course of your life in learning to keep in step with the Spirit? Give an example.

3. Suffering as Jesus suffered is a crucial ingredient in the process of becoming a holy person. How has such suffering been tied to resisting temptation in your life? Do you need to ask for prayer that you will remain faithful through your suffering?

Chapter Seven

Holiness Is Proven by Its Justice

FEW MATTERS ARE AS controversial in the evangelical wing of the American church today as questions of social justice, or what is nowadays referred to as "wokeness." In fact, Owen Strachan, author of the book *Christianity and Wokeness: How the Social Justice Movement is Hijacking the Gospel—and the Way to Stop It*, states that "wokeness is a major threat to the Christian church."[1] "Wokeness is anti-Gospel."[2] He finally urges that wokeness advocates ought to be excommunicated, that is expelled from the body of Christ.[3] But how exactly learning a thing or two from the field of critical race theory, or working to sharpen the church's concern for justice, mercy, and equity in our communities, how any of these things pose "a major threat" to the gospel of Jesus Christ is far from obvious to me—even after reading Dr. Strachan's book.[4]

According to Scripture, holiness and justice go together like soup and a sandwich. Yahweh's declaration through the prophet Amos is paradigmatic: "Let justice roll on like a river, righteousness like a never-failing stream" (5:24). The psalmist extols the

---

1. Strachan, *Christianity and Wokeness*, 2.
2. Strachan, *Christianity and Wokeness*, 51.
3. Strachan, *Christianity and Wokeness*, 54.
4. Strachan does allow for biblical justice in opposition to social justice, but as I intend to show in this chapter, social justice is an important component of biblical justice.

connection between the Lord's holiness and his passion for just and righteous dealings among his people:

> Great is the LORD in Zion;
> He is exalted over all the nations.
> Let them praise your great and awesome name—
> He is holy.
> The king is mighty, he loves justice—
> You have established equity. (Ps 99:2–4)

The Holy One loves justice! That statement ought to sink deeply into our hearts and minds.[5]

These two passages barely scratch the surface of the voluminous biblical pairing of holiness with a passion for justice in human affairs. But why is this the case? Why should holiness *by definition* entail the concern to see justice and righteousness prevail in all relationships?

Let's begin by defining a few terms. What is justice? And how is it determined? For the purposes of this book, it will be sufficient to think of justice *as ensuring that a person receives the treatment that he or she deserves*. Deciding what kind of treatment a person deserves is in turn related to several key factors: the nature of humanity; living attentively to the relational expectations of life in the kingdom of God; and the legal expectations that are being applied.

First, as we consider the nature of humanity as we think about justice, we need to remember that all people are created as the image of God, a doctrine still often referred to in its Latin form as the *imago Dei*. Because of this all people deserve to be treated with the dignity and respect due to a divine representative. Because everyone bears God's image, every single person is always more than the worst thing they have ever done, deserving of dignity and respect. Nothing can remove or destroy God's image.[6] Therefore, any be-

---

5. Also notice the synonymous parallelism between justice and equity. To be synonymous means that the two words mean basically the same thing. This is significant because the idea of social equity has also become a bad idea among some evangelicals.

6. Despite a long theological tradition that says otherwise, there is no

havior that mistreats a person in any way for whatever reason; any behavior that dehumanizes a person, as happens when someone is tortured, kept in solitary confinement, ridiculed, abused or discriminated against, is always unjust. We abuse the image of God by mistreating people in these ways.

Second, it is significant that justice and righteousness are overlapping terms in Scripture. For example, notice again the poetic, synonymous parallelism between these two words in Amos 5:24: "Let justice roll on like a river, righteousness like a never-failing stream." *Synonymous* means that these are two words that say similar things. In the New Testament the word *dikaiosunē* can be translated as either righteousness or justice. Furthermore, *dikaiosunē* is defined relationally. That is, I am judged to be righteous or just according to how carefully I adhere to the proper requirements and expectations of my relationships (whether collectively or individually). For the people of Israel, those relational expectations are defined by adherence to God's law. For instance, the Gospel of Luke describes Zechariah and Elizabeth, parents of John the Baptist, as "righteous/just in the sight of God" because they "observe all the Lord's commands and decrees blamelessly" (Luke 1:6). Obeying God's word keeps all dimensions of their relational lives properly ordered, just and righteous.

The New Testament consistently demonstrates that the definition of justice is fundamentally relational. We also see the conceptual overlap between justice and righteousness as it plays out in various places. In the Sermon on the Mount, for example, Jesus pronounces a blessing upon all "those who hunger and thirst for justice (*dikaiosunē*)" (Matt 5:6). According to Jesus, the kingdom of God belongs to "those who are persecuted because of their hunger for justice (*dikaiosunē*)" (Matt 5:10). Maintaining right relationships, expressed as a hunger for justice, is now defined around Jesus and membership in the kingdom of God.[7]

---

biblical warrant for the idea that the *imago Dei* was broken, warped, or eliminated by humanity's fall into sin.

7. For an exposition of the kingdom ethics taught by Jesus, see my book *I Pledge Allegiance*.

Third, we cannot escape that our discussion about righteousness and justice presupposes a specific standard for judging an individual as just or righteous. We cannot arbitrarily decide matters of justice and fairness. Only the Creator can decide what constitutes fairness, equity, and right relationship in his creation. The Holy One has given us definite instructions for what he desires from us. For the Christian today, our standards of justice and righteousness are determined by the Holy One's own character and expectations provided in God's revelation to us, now in Scripture. Jesus states this very clearly when he repeats Yahweh's declaration pronounced at Mount Sinai: "all those who love me keep my commandments" (Exod 20:6; Deut 5:10; Dan 9:4; John 14:15). Obeying God's instructions is the spontaneous fruit of genuine love for the Holy One. Talk of love without obedience is nothing but empty words, reminiscent of a rain cloud whose moisture peters out before it touches the ground.

The Reciprocity of Love

Repeatedly the Old and New Testaments declare the Holy One's concern for the *reciprocity of love*. Deuteronomy 6:5 reminded the Israelites that the heart of the covenant was to "love the LORD your God with all your heart, with all your soul, and all your strength." In addition, Leviticus 19:18 included the command to "love your neighbor as yourself. For I am the LORD." Jesus combined these two commands into the New Testament "Wikipedia" version summarizing all of God's law as: "Love the Lord your God with all your heart and with all your soul and with all your mind and with all your strength. The second is this: Love your neighbor as yourself. There is no commandment greater than these" (Mark 12:30–31; also see Gal 5:14; Jas 2:8).

Loving God and one another remain the core of divine justice throughout Scripture. Also notice that loving others is intimately connected in many texts with a genuine love for God. In the words of the apostle James: "Religion that God our Father accepts as pure and faultless is this: to look after orphans and widows in their distress and to keep oneself from being polluted by the world" (Jas 1:27). Justice and personal morality, i.e., individual holiness, go hand in hand because they are two sides of the same coin, each associated with the other.

To Love My Neighbor as Myself

We have come full circle. We return as we began to the one who is Wholly Other. God can only be known insofar as God chooses to reveal himself. Knowing the Holy One is the miraculously possible impossibility, for it is seeing the invisible God, being welcomed into the divine mystery. Trusting in God's revelation requires accepting the lessons only God can teach us. Foundational to these divine lessons is the fact that God's holiness makes him the God of redemption; the God who rescued Israel from slavery; the God who sacrificed his only Son on the cross for humanity's salvation. This holy God is always our Savior God *who loves us and sacrifices for us*, displaying his love in just and righteous relationships.

Here is the biblical standard for justice and righteousness. *I must love God completely.* How do I love God? By obeying his commandments. What is God's greatest commandment? To love my neighbor as myself. Therefore, whatever I would righteously wish to have or to experience for myself (so, excluding our fallen, wicked desires) is always the standard for how I should justly and righteously treat my neighbor. This is the gold standard for justice in Scripture and in God's world.

If I do not want to be oppressed, then I must work to see that my neighbor is not oppressed, by myself or anyone else. If my neighbor is already being oppressed, then I am compelled to remove that oppression.

If I do not like being discriminated against, then I cannot discriminate against my neighbor. And I must work to alleviate any discrimination that may already exist.

If I do not want to live a hungry, impoverished life, then I must work to ensure that my neighbor is never abandoned to poverty or hunger, without prospects for food or resources.

If I do not want to be abandoned or alone, then I must ensure that my neighbor is not abandoned or left alone to fend for herself.

The point is clear, I hope, and can easily be extended by the reader imagining any number of concrete realities whose privation one would sorely experience; this then becomes a front for working for justice in God's world.

By living a life of sacrificial servanthood dedicated to relieving the suffering of others, we demonstrate that we are a holy people emulating our Savior God. For sacrificial servanthood is exactly the type of behavior that Yahweh revealed to Israel and that Jesus Christ reveals to his disciples in bringing the kingdom of God in his life and ministry. The Holy One has done everything possible to love his neighbor—you and me. Now we are called to demonstrate our holiness by being like him in loving justice and doing everything possible to love our neighbor.

The Scriptures are replete with stories that describe the lengths to which God is willing to go in order to bring justice to his people as well as to the surrounding nations. The following is only a smattering of these texts:

- Leviticus 19 is a lengthy combination of moral and ceremonial commands, many dealing with justice, all fulfilling the command, "Be holy because I the LORD your God am holy" (verse 1).
- Psalm 99:4, the mighty King loves justice and equity.
- Psalm 68:4–6, the Holy One is father to the fatherless, defender of widows.
- Psalm 72:12–14, the LORD delivers the needy and afflicted; he rescues them from affliction and violence.
- Psalm 140:12, the LORD secures justice for the poor, upholding the cause of the needy.
- Proverbs 29:7, "The righteous care about justice for the poor, but the wicked have no such concern."

- Isaiah 1:16–17, "Learn to do right; seek justice. Defend the oppressed. Take up the cause of the fatherless; plead the case of the widow."
- Isaiah 5:16, "But the Lord Almighty will be exalted by his justice, and the holy God will be proved holy by his righteous acts."
- Isaiah 11:4, "with righteousness he will judge the needy, with justice he will give decisions for the poor of the earth."
- Isaiah 61:8, "For I, the Lord, love justice."
- Matthew 12:18–20, the Servant Messiah will proclaim justice to the nations, leading justice to victory.
- Luke 3:10–14, John the Baptist commands people to share with the poor and to treat everyone fairly.
- Luke 11:42, the Pharisees are warned of impending judgment because they "neglect justice and the love of God."

Although the Holy One's concern for justice begins with a focus on relationships among the covenant people, God's desire for justice is not limited to members of the covenant community. God's concerns are not so insular. On several occasions Yahweh condemns disobedient Israel for being discriminatory and withholding justice from the non-Israelites (referred to as aliens) living among them (Deut 24:17; Ezek 22:29; Mal 3:5). We cannot pick and choose who is worthy of our compassion based on tribalistic, racial, or exclusionary measures. All human beings bear the *imago Dei*. The Holy One insisted that even the foreigner who was most unlike God's covenant people was still deserving of just, righteous treatment. God does not show such favoritism and neither should his people (Acts 10:34; Rom 2:11; Eph 6:9; Col 3:25 Jas 2:1, 9).

Everyone is worthy of love and all that flows from loving. The prophet Isaiah expresses Yahweh's desire to bring justice to all the nations of the earth (Isa 42 1; 51:5). The covenant people may be the centerpiece of God's attention but his interests in seeing "justice roll down" like a divine flood washing away all unfairness, inequity, and suffering extends to everyone everywhere.

Hidden Holiness

The Problem of American Individualism

One of the reasons that some American evangelicals remain hostile to ideas of social justice, or wokeness, is because of the American love affair with rugged individualism. Unfortunately, a single-minded concern with individual salvation and all that it entails—personal repentance, individual responsibility, personal sanctification—can blind us to the collective guilt of societal sins requiring a collective, societal response. Neither the personal nor the collective dimensions of sin in this world cancel each other out. Both are important to recognize, and both must be dealt with on their own terms.

Any human society, and thus any society being built by sinners, will produce a mixed bag of both beautiful and terrible results. The image of God shines through in many humane, creative elements of our various cultures. But equally, the cumulative effects of the various sinful contributions made by sinful social architects will also produce numerous instances of systemic problems and injustices—unjust laws, discriminatory hierarchies, and indifference to the needy and the powerless. Thus, seemingly intractable problems such as systemic, structural racism (to name only one) become a fact of life.[8] Addressing the world's social problems therefore requires a two-pronged approach. On the one hand, transforming individual hearts and minds is always key to a genuine reformation of a deeply ingrained social injustice. As an evangelical Christian, I agree that personal repentance for sin, trust in Jesus Christ as Savior and Lord, accompanied by genuine discipleship as a citizen in the kingdom of God are all essential for the life of the Christian church. On the other hand, personal renewal does not negate the need for critical legislative reform. We need both if we are to see a measure of justice in this world. Creating new laws that seek to reorganize unjust power structures, legislating for equity (that is, equal opportunity, not necessarily equal

---

8. For an exhaustive, and exhausting, historical investigation into the problem of systemic racism in American society, see Rothstein, *Color of Law*. Anyone who can read this book yet still deny the existence of structural racism and its long-term consequences in America has not been paying attention.

outcomes), and building mechanisms of ubiquitous charity—yes, charity and generosity—into our social fabric are also essential.

In fact, building such a two-pronged system of social justice was God's own strategy as outlined in Scripture. The Old Testament describes an extensive welfare system for the people of Israel that required individuals to act for the greater good in ways that would (ideally) align with their most holy personal desires. In this respect, holiness was legislated from the top down; it was not only a matter of personal responsibility but also *a social obligation determined by law*. Even though we are separated from the Old Testament environment(s) by vast differences in time and customs, we can still learn about the Holy One's priorities for a society pleasing to God, drawing relevant principles for contemporary Christian decision-making in the public square. In Scripture, we learn about God's values in both personal and social ethics as well as national decision-making regarding the treatment of the poor, the indigent, immigrants, and the use of personal property.

The story of ancient Israel describes the one time in history when God wrote a nation's legislation; Israel was a theocracy. Breaking Old Testament law was transgression against the LORD. A good deal of the Old Testament prophetic critique against Israel arose from the people's failure to implement God's social welfare legislation (Isa 3:13–15; 10:1–2; 58:6–10; Jer 22:1–5; Amos 5:11–12). Although neither the USA nor the modern church are today's equivalents of ancient Israel, God's priorities for holy justice in this world have not changed. We ought to pay attention to biblical texts of justice in both Old and New Testaments, and respond appropriately. Though I do not see a New Testament mandate obligating the church deliberately to transform secular society—to redeem the world, as some would say—I do see far-reaching possibilities for the Holy Spirit's direction as God's people strive creatively to love their neighbors as themselves in every dimension of personal and public life.

Reading Scripture, we can easily observe that *the Holy One hates poverty*, which is another way of saying he despises inequity.[9]

9. See the chapter titled "God Hates Poverty" in my *I Pledge Allegiance*.

After instructing Israel to cancel all debts every seven years, Deuteronomy 15:4 concludes that *"there should be no poor people among you."* If it happens that some people do become poor, as seems inevitable in this world (Deut 15:11), then God's people are to "be open handed and freely lend him [the poor person] whatever he needs" without judgment or criticism (Deut 15:8; also see Exod 23:10–12; Lev 25:1–7, 8–17). God commanded a system of checks and balances (loan forgiveness every seven years) with a large safety net encompassing all of society (guaranteed charity for everyone who needed it). In fact, as we will see, charity is emphasized so strongly throughout this legislation that not only are the rich *obligated* to care for the poor but the poor have *a right* to expect charity from the rich. Isaiah 10:2 explicitly condemns Israel's leaders for "depriving the poor of *their rights* by withholding justice." That's holy justice.

Yahweh regularly reminds Israel that everything they had belongs to him and came to them as his generous gift. In this biblical ethic, private property is never truly private. God has the right to tell us what to do with our property. And what he tells us is that *we* must share our property, share it all generously. Every farmer knew that he was not growing crops for himself and his family alone. He was growing crops for the entire community. Each individual's harvest was also a community harvest to be shared. Below is a brief list of only some of this biblical legislation:

- Every seventh year all fields, vineyards, and orchards were to remain unharvested; all the produce of that year was available for the poor to take for themselves (Exod 23:10–12; Lev 25:1–7).
- Landowners were never to harvest all of a crop for themselves; *a portion of every crop was being grown for the poor.* A margin of unharvested grain was to be left around the edges of every field; the poor were free to harvest what they needed (Lev 19:9–10).

Holiness Is Proven by Its Justice

- Anyone could enter a farmer's field, vineyard, or orchard at any time and freely eat as much as their hands could carry (Deut 23:24–25; see Mark 2:23–24).
- Whatever fell to the ground during harvest, whether in a field, a vineyard, or an orchard, could not be picked up; it must be left for the poor and the wild animals (Deut 24:19–20).
- Farmers could only harvest once; anything that grew or matured after the first harvest must be left for the poor (Deut 24:20–22).
- Every fifty years, during the Year of Jubilee, all debts were canceled, all fields were left fallow, all vineyards and orchards went untouched, so that the poor could harvest the crops; and all real estate was returned to the original owner (Lev 25:8–17).

A great deal more could be said about Israel's social welfare laws, but space prevents a fuller treatment here.[10] God's priorities, however, are already clear. *God called his people to become an equitable, just society sustained through the redistribution of wealth.* This is what some today would call distributive justice.[11] The Holy One set quantitative limits and time constraints on both the accumulation of wealth and the desperation of poverty. The rich could only remain unusually wealthy for so long. Fifty years to be exact. The poor would only remain in poverty for the same length of time. Every fifty years the LORD required that Israel hit the reset button in order to recreate a society of equality as originally intended. All real estate returned to the families, clans, and tribes that had owned it originally. Multigenerational wealth and poverty, where the haves and the have-nots grow further and further apart over the decades, was not permitted among God's people—at least, when they were an obedient and holy people. This was God's vision of a just society. Charity was prioritized over efficiency,

10. For a good treatment of these issues in greater detail, see Keller, *Generous Justice*.

11. Contrary to Strachan, who says, "Biblical justice is not *distributive*"; *Christianity and Wokeness*, 97.

generosity over material success, community over individualism, and equity for all people over personal accumulation.

Biblical Justice and the Church

The Christian church should be the epicenter of divine justice today. The Holy One has always intended that the people of God reflect the Edenic ideals that were lost after creation's corruption by sin, as we read in the first few chapters of the book of Genesis. The church is the heart of God's new creation. It is called to be a new kind of community that banishes favoritism and inequity from its ranks (Jas 2:1–7). Poor folk cannot sit and worship Jesus alongside wealthy folk on Sunday morning only to be ignored and neglected by their rich brothers and sisters throughout the rest of the week. Responsible church leadership will find creative ways to implement equitable relationships among all members of the body of Christ.

The New Testament church well understood these Old Testament lessons, voluntarily implementing the Holy One's expectations for justice among his people. Acts 2:44–45 tells us that "all the believers were together and had everything in common. Selling their possessions and goods, they gave to anyone as he had need." Deliberately referring back to God's charge in Deuteronomy 15:4 that "there were to be no poor people among them," Acts 4:32–35 says, "All the believers were one in heart and mind. No one claimed that any of his possessions was his own, but they shared everything they had . . . There were no needy persons among them. For from time to time those who owned lands or houses sold them, brought the money from the sales and put it at the apostles' feet and it was distributed to anyone as he had need."[12]

But God's holy people will see that their passion for justice does not stop at the church door. It must spill out into the broader community, seeping into society at large. Like the Holy One, we too will want to see justice roll down like a torrential stream,

---

12. See my treatment of these issues in *I Pledge Allegiance*, 152–70.

bringing righteous relationships to every sector of society—in race relationships, financial dealings, environmental problems,[13] and more. This, too, is a part of the history of the Christian church. One dramatic, early example illustrating the wide-ranging influence of Christian social concern erupted in AD 362 when the Roman emperor Julian complained about the general public's growing neglect of the traditional Roman gods. The problem, in Julian's eyes, was the extraordinarily generous levels of public benevolence shown to the poor by the Christian church all throughout the empire.[14] The church was undermining pagan devotion and illuminating the love of Christ by acting out God's concerns for social justice in all the world.

My purpose is not to imply that Christians should limit themselves to private charitable organizations functioning only through the local church. Not at all. Unlike the early church, we enjoy the benefits of living in a society that allows public participation in the administrative and legislative circles of government. It is possible to bring a Christian conscience about social justice to bear on rewriting laws and deconstructing unjust hierarchies that stand in the way of true justice and equity in our communities and the wider world.

Looking Ahead to Retributive Justice

An attentive reader will have noticed that there is one aspect of biblical justice that I have not discussed so far. This is the harsher side of justice: the part of divine justice that punishes wrongdoing and calls sinners to repentance. This aspect of justice is sometimes called *retributive justice* because it brings *retribution*, i.e., punishment, down upon the unjust. The Old Testament prophets warned Israel of the Holy One's impending retribution when he threatened them with Assyrian and Babylonian exile. One of Israel's principal

---

13. Though I have not talked about this issue here, the Old Testament social welfare laws gives considerable attention to Israel's responsibility to care for the environment and its animal life; for example, see Exod 23:11–12.

14. Cited in Bell, *Economy of Desire*, 198.

Hidden Holiness

sins was its failure to consistently abide by God's social welfare laws; the nation's habit of neglecting and mistreating the poor, the fatherless and the widow is a repeated refrain in Yahweh's condemnation of apostate Israel. The New Testament apostle James repeats a similar message when he exhorts the Jerusalem church to "speak and act as those who are going to be judged by the law that gives freedom, because judgment without mercy will be shown to anyone who has not been merciful. Mercy triumphs over judgment" (2:12–13).

"Judgment without mercy will be shown to anyone who has not been merciful." In other words, God's retributive justice searches out evidence of distributive justice in human affairs and judges accordingly. With that in mind, it is now time to look at the retributive side of justice from the perspective of the Holy One. We will do this in the final chapter of this book.

Discussion Questions:

1. The chapter argues that holiness cannot be separated from the quest for justice. Explain how these two are connected. Why is a holy God—and his holy people—passionate about justice in human affairs?

2. It is clear that the biblical vision of justice is at odds with important elements of American culture and values. Explain the various issues at stake. What do these contrasts means for a Christian's witness in this world?

3. In how many different ways must an obedient American Christian church (and you as an individual) be countercultural in the pursuit of holiness? Spell them out. What can this alternative lifestyle look like in your church today? What practical steps can you take to implement the necessary changes in your congregational life?

Chapter Eight

Holiness, History, and the End of It All

AVID READERS ARE USUALLY eager to get to the end of a good mystery novel. Some eager beavers will even cheat by skipping ahead to consume the last chapter first. They want to know in advance where the story is headed. Was it the butler in the drawing room who murdered the lord of the manor, or was it the weekend guest with the derringer in his pocket? By knowing the ending ahead of time, a reader can guess what pieces of evidence to look for as the story unfolds.

I prefer to stay up late into the wee hours of the morning on marathon reading binges so that I can gather the evidence chapter by chapter, while still cutting back my waiting time for the denouement. Can I follow the trail of evidence to the proper conclusions, or is the author trying to misdirect me? Can I fit the pieces together or is the writer playing fast and loose with the plotline? There is nothing worse than a dramatic conclusion that drops out of thin air into a plot that never hinted at any such thing. Introducing the guilty party as a new character, unconnected to anything that has gone before, in the last ten pages of the book is lazy writing that cheats the reader of the satisfaction of figuring it out for themselves.

Hidden Holiness

As God inspired and directed the Bible's creation, attentive readers will see that there is no evidence of laziness nor that readers are being cheated. The Bible tells the epic story about the Creator's work in the history of his creation. For those readers eager to learn about the end of the story, there is no need to wait till the climax erupts in the book of Revelation—the last book of the Bible. Not everyone will like the Bible's conclusion, but at least it doesn't trick us with an ending unrelated to the rest of the plot. In fact, a number of New Testament authors help the eager reader skip ahead in the timeline, learning about history's conclusion long before the Bible's concluding book weaves it all together. There may not be an excess of details, but we are given ample time to see how the pieces of the storyline will fall together.

The final chapter of God's work in history is revealed in broad brushstrokes. For instance, Mark 13:26–27 tells us, "At that time [the end of history] people will see the Son of Man [Jesus] coming in clouds with great power and glory. And he will send his angels and gather his elect from the four winds, from the ends of the earth to the ends of the heaven." We might wish for more details, but we are clearly told that history ends with a new beginning, the return of the glorified, empowered, resurrected Jesus to rule over the heavens and the earth with all of his chosen people.

How does the theme of holiness fit into this final dénouement?

On the one hand, we may expect nothing different at all. God has always been holy; God will always be holy. The Wholly Other is the same yesterday, today, and forever. Holiness never changes.

On the other hand, God's historical engagement with humanity has highlighted a number of important traits that we can now see as central to divine holiness. Holiness never changes, but God's historical interactions with human beings teach us about the contours of divine holiness in greater detail. Seeing those inner workings requires revelation.

From this revelation we learn that the Holy One is not only Wholly Other, distinguished from creation by an Infinite Qualitative Difference, but we also learn that the Holy One wants to reveal himself to us. He is a God of self-disclosure who wants personal relationships. God is not content to commune with himself, even though he needs nothing more. The Holy One is a relational God who wants to engage in intimate, personal connection with human beings. As God moves to show himself to us, we learn that the Holy One is motivated by grace—that is, a commitment to take the initiative, to build bridges where none existed before towards people who do not deserve God's attention. So, the One who is Wholly Other sent a savior to redeem humanity from slavery to sin; his one and only Son came to die on a Roman cross. In addition, God sent the gift of the Holy Spirit, empowering his people to participate in divine holiness themselves. The Holy One created a holy people who are empowered to grow in personal holiness as they prepare to meet God personally, face to face at the end of time.

Becoming holy means living a life characterized by continual, heartfelt adoration for the insuperable majesty of the Holy One. Holy people are worshiping people, adoring people. A habit of extolling God's holiness instils character shaped by divine love and the fruit of the Holy Spirit. Loving God with all our heart, soul, mind, and strength, as well as loving our neighbor as ourself, is the core of Spirit-empowered holiness. The fruit of the Spirit thus shapes holy people to display love, joy, peace, patience, gentleness, goodness, faith, meekness, and self-control (Gal 5:22–23). Such godly character is passionate about pursuing justice for others in an unjust, unholy world, serving the oppressed neighbor as the Holy One has served us.

Since justice is an expression of God's holiness, holy justice not only entails the type of merciful, distributive justice described in chapter 7. It also involves, with equal measure, the judicial quality of *retributive* justice: that is, moral retribution, punishment for wrongdoing, judgment against the guilty and unrepentant. The guarantee of retributive justice meted out by the Holy One is not limited to the Old Testament depiction of God. This judicial characteristic is firmly entrenched in the New Testament as well and cannot be overlooked. Paul urges the Roman church to leave issues of final judgment with God rather than taking matters into their own hands. The Holy One can be trusted to adjudicate all concerns fairly when the final judgment eventually arrives. Quoting from Deuteronomy 32:35, the apostle Paul presses home the lesson of loving our neighbors, including our enemies, by saying, "Do not take revenge, my friends, but leave room for God's wrath, for it is written: 'It is mine to avenge; I will repay,' says the Lord'" (Rom 12:19). It's God's role to judge and condemn. It's our role to love unconditionally as God has loved us. God's holy wrath is God's alone to administer, and it is always directed expertly with a comprehensive understanding of where, why and how it is the only appropriate final resort to the human predicament.

God's wrath is the divine manifestation of holy condemnation and eternal punishment meted out against human rebelliousness and personal sin (Eph 5:6; Col 3:6; 1 Thess 2:16). The only avenue for avoiding God's wrath, and instead receiving the eternal blessings of God's salvation, is to trust in the Lord Jesus Christ, appropriate his redemption, and walk in the Spirit-empowered purity of faith, hope, and love (1 Thess 5:1–11, especially verse 9).

The Measure of God's Judgment

Central to the biblical notion of retributive justice is the fact that God pays attention to how his people are treated by others. Unfortunately, life in this fallen world frequently ensures that disobedience against God can be accompanied by hostility towards God's people. As Jesus warned his disciples, "If the world hates you, keep in mind that it hated me first" (John 15:18). Rejecting Jesus easily expresses itself in the rejection and ridicule of Jesus' followers. The history of suffering and martyrdom for the Christian church reminds us of the high price often exacted for a believer's faithfulness to Jesus Christ. In fact, 2 Timothy 3:12 reminds us that "everyone who wants to live a godly life in Christ Jesus will be persecuted." Yet, God's people can take encouragement from the New Testament promise that none of this opposition passes God's notice. The Holy One sees it all and keeps a record not because he is vindictive but because he is just.

Holiness, History, and the End of It All

The book of Revelation assures us that God will avenge the suffering of his people. After God destroys the whore of Babylon in Revelation 18, depicting the all-encompassing, systemic evils of godless, bloody, exploitative, human empires, a chorus of praise erupts in chapter 19, declaring that "true and just are God's judgments" (verse 2a). The principal evidence of God's true justice is the fact that "he has avenged on her (the whore of Babylon) the blood of his servants" (verse 2d). Here is the final answer to the repeated prayers of God's persecuted saints pleading in chapter 6, "How long, sovereign Lord, holy and true, until you judge the inhabitants of the earth and avenge our blood?" (verse 10). Though God keeps his people waiting until his timing is fulfilled, the message is clear: the Holy One will one day avenge the cruel injustices suffered by his saints on Christ's behalf. Just as Yahweh heard the cries for help and saw the years of suffering endured by the people of Israel in Exodus 3:7-10, so the Holy One continues to see the suffering and hear the laments of his chosen people. The ultimate execution of holy justice is finally described in Revelation 19:15c, where the exalted Christ "treads the winepress of the fury of the wrath of God Almighty" (also Rev 14:19). Humanity's savior and redeemer will eventually become the Father's wrathful executioner who punishes the sins of a rebellious world.

The apostle Paul shared this belief in God's retributive justice measuring out condemnation and punishment upon those who have rejected the gospel of Jesus Christ and opposed the Spirit-filled messengers commissioned by God to share this good news. Paul briefly refers to God's punishment of his personal opponents in 1 Thessalonians 2:16. Their efforts to stop Paul's ministry have "heaped up their sins to the limit. The wrath of God has come upon them at last." Paul's proleptic description of final judgment—note that God's wrath has already come upon them; their judgment has already occurred—highlights the inevitable connection between (a) current opposition to the gospel with (b) impending condemnation at the end of time.

Paul's most elaborate description of the final judgment appears in his second letter to the Thessalonian church. Whether we like it or not, we can't help but notice the explicit connection made in 2 Thessalonians between the claim that "God is just" and his commitment to settling the accounts of his people through judgment and punishment:

> All this is evidence that *God's judgment is right*, and as a result you will be counted worthy of the kingdom of God, for which you are suffering. *God is just*: He will pay back trouble to those who trouble you and give relief to you who are troubled, and to us as well. This will happen when the Lord Jesus is revealed from heaven in blazing fire with his powerful angels. He will punish those who do not know God and do not obey the gospel of our Lord Jesus. They will be punished with everlasting destruction and shut out from the presence of the Lord and from the glory of his might on the day he comes to be glorified in his holy people and to be marveled at among all those who have believed. This includes you, because you believed our testimony to you. (2 Thess 1:5–10)

"Everlasting destruction" consists of being "shut out of the Lord's presence" for all of eternity. In the end, God's justice will give us what we wanted. Those who received Jesus Christ will thrive as they bask in the never-ending glory of God. Those who choose to reject the Holy One and his one and only Son will be rejected themselves, consigned to exist apart from the very source of their existence. Until this final moment arrives, no human being will have ever experienced the full measure of existential torment of what it means to exist apart from the source and meaning of our existence, to be isolated from the only hope we have of discovering our deepest satisfactions in life.

The Father of life makes himself continually available to everyone for as long as they live. "He causes the sun to rise on the evil and the good, and sends rain on the righteous and the unrighteous," providing life and sustenance to everyone regardless of their personal disposition towards him (Matt 5:45). The final judgment will bring about a new state of alienated existence for condemned sinners, an unprecedented condition never experienced by anyone before. It will be the emptiness, the eternal darkness of being cut off once and for all from the glorious existence that could have been, that was hinted at even in the rebellious life that was lived in opposition to God. Once an opponent loses the object of his opposition, what does he become? Nothing but an empty cipher. An empty cipher with a hyperactive conscience forever screaming self-condemnation in the darkness.

Perhaps the most poignant depiction of eternal judgment, specifying the direct connection between the outcome of God's retributive justice and the treatment of God's people in this world, is found in one of the most misunderstood passages of the New Testament—Jesus' story of the sheep and the goats in Matthew 25:31–46. The meaning of this story hinges on how we identify the group that Jesus refers to as "the least of these brothers of mine" (verses 40, 45), for the entire human race is finally divided according to the treatment given to this group of people.

The least of these has often been understood as a reference to the world's poor and destitute, making the final judgment a referendum on personal acts of charity and humanitarianism. To look into the eyes of the poor is to stare into the face of Jesus, according to this view. Mother Theresa of Calcutta was famous for using this passage to explain her ministry to the most despised, poverty-stricken segments of Indian society. However, as vitally important as anyone's service to the poor may be, this particular reading of Matthew 25 must be challenged. Like any piece of literature, the Gospel of Matthew ought to be read as a literary whole with its own narrative continuity and thematic consistency. The question is not what we think "the least of these brothers of mine" might mean but what the Gospel of Matthew indicates the phrase means. What interpretive clues does Matthew offer for the most contextually appropriate interpretation of the phrase?

If we study the whole of Matthew carefully, it will become clear that the least of Jesus' brothers can only refer to Christ's disciples who have been engaged in proclaiming the kingdom of God. Each of the descriptors used—the least of these, my brothers, those who are dependent on the generosity of others, those who need to be visited in prison, and Jesus' promise that anyone who receives you receives me—are all applied *to the disciples* as they travel the world announcing the good news of Jesus Christ and God's kingdom (see Matt 10:11–20, 40–42; 12:48–50; 18:2–6). Matthew is not offering a cart blanche description of Jesus' spiritual identification with the world's poor. Far from it. The sheep are all those who have welcomed the disciples and their gospel message with hospitality, offering room and board, financial support, and even visited the disciples in prison after the ruling authorities have tried to squelch their preaching. The goats, on the other hand, are the hostile portion of the world who rejects Jesus and, thus, rejects his people and their gospel message. They refused to help God's people because they were often the persecutors oppressing Jesus' disciples and throwing them into prison.

Thus, the world's treatment of the church becomes the measuring rod for determining the world's judgment. The sheep, those who received Jesus and assisted his people, are blessed by the Father; they receive an inheritance—"the kingdom prepared since the creation of the world" (verse 34). The goats, those who rejected Jesus and ignored or oppressed God's people, are cursed. To them Jesus says, "Depart from me into the eternal fire prepared for the devil and his angels" (verse 41). The consistency in these New Testament themes of final judgment is noteworthy. Horrific agony is again connected to separation from God. And the Holy One's identification with his people is so complete that whatever is done to the saints is done to the Savior. The world's treatment of the church determines God's judgment of the world.

Glorification Through Judgment

From a human vantage point, perhaps the most remarkable aspect of the final judgment is the fact that the Holy One is glorified through his execution of holy wrath. Perhaps the damned themselves will fall down and bless the Lord on that day as they acknowledge the true justice of their well-merited condemnation. Allow me to cite a lengthy passage from the book of Revelation that underscores the praise and adoration due to God for his righteous judgment. Upon the completion of God's wrath poured out against the wicked (Rev 15:1) a heavenly chorus sings out:

> "Great and marvelous are your deeds,
> > Lord God Almighty.
> Just and true are your ways,
> > King of the nations.
> Who will not fear you, Lord,
> > and bring glory to your name?
> For you alone are holy.
> All nations will come
> > and worship before you,
> > for your righteous acts have been revealed." (Rev 15:3–4)

> "You are just in these judgments, O Holy One,
> > you who are and who were;
> for they have shed the blood of your holy people and your prophets,
> > and you have given them blood to drink as they deserve."
> And I heard the altar respond:
> "Yes, Lord God Almighty,
> > true and just are your judgments." (Rev 16:5–7)

True and just are the judgments of the Holy One. Rectifying history's wrongs and condemning the evils of human rebelliousness with eternal punishment all bring glory to God. And even though our study has covered considerable ground, we cannot forget our starting point in the Lord's Prayer. The Lord's Prayer should make every disciple pray with fervent desire for *God to glorify himself,* to reveal his almighty holiness before the watching world. Recall the important background to that request in the prophet Ezekiel where Yahweh repeatedly promises to redeem his people Israel *for his own sake,* for the glory of his great name.

New Testament believers need to remember this lesson as we enjoy the blessings of our salvation today. Yes, the Holy One wants to bless us. We receive tremendous benefits from all of the Father's work on our behalf, whether it be the gift of salvation through Jesus' work on the cross or the final judgment where the Lord defends his people and condemns the wicked. But the more important goal for all of God's works is the Holy One's self-glorification. This includes divine judgment, which, for the purposes of God's glory, must include the church as well as the church's opponents. We have already seen Peter's assurance that God's judgment must begin with the church (1 Pet 4:17)! Similarly, Paul tells the Corinthians that "we all must appear before the judgment seat of Christ, so that each of us may receive what is due to us for the things done while in the body, whether good or bad" (2 Cor 5:10).

No one is exempt.

Yet, this is also where we learn about the difference between judgment and condemnation. While no one is exempt from the first, God's people will be spared the second. First Corinthians 3:13–15 offers Paul's most dramatic image of this distinction. In this passage the fire of eternal judgment "will test the quality of each person's work." Everything that survives the fire will be rewarded, while the rest is counted as a total loss *except* for the individual believer who will still be saved—"even though only as one escaping through the flames" (verse 15). In other words, we will all be judged, but God's people are never condemned.

The final judgment is described similarly in the book of Revelation (20:11–15; 22:12). On the one hand, everyone without exception will be judged, weighed and measured "according to what they had done as recorded in the books" (20:12c, 13c; 22:12).[1] Humanity will then be divided. There is another book (singular) that stands in contrast to the books (plural) that have recorded human achievements. This book is called the book of life; it records the names of all those who trust Jesus Christ as resurrected Lord and Savior. "If anyone's name was not found written in the book of life, he was thrown into the lake of fire" (20:15).

Why is the story of final judgment told in this way?

First, it is clear that each and every person, Christians included, will be judged by God according to "what they have done." In this respect, everyone's account falls short. When judged according

---

1. Jewish apocalyptic literature at the time imagined heavenly record keepers who transcribed the events of each person's life, holding onto the records for judgment day. This is the background to "the books" mentioned in Revelation.

to our performance, accomplishments, and failures, no one's life proves satisfactory or acceptable to the Holy One. This reckoning with the heavenly books proves once and for all that everyone falls short of God's righteous expectations. No one is righteous, no not one. No one deserves redemption in and of themselves. No one measures up to God's glory. Everyone deserves condemnation in the lake of fire, including those who have cast their lot with the crucified, resurrected Lamb of God. We will finally see this clearly for ourselves without dissimulation.

This conclusion is all the more remarkable given the fact that God's people are promised a glorious reward when Christ appears (1 Pet 5:4, 10; also 1 Cor 15:43; 2 Cor 3:18; 4:17; 2 Thess 1:10; 2:14). Obviously, the Christian's reception of heavenly glory (whatever form that takes) is also a complete gift, even if it is commensurate with our sanctified status as saints walking in the power of the Spirit. The only people to escape condemnation are those whose names are inscribed by Jesus' own nail-pierced hand into the Lamb's book of life. It does not matter how many rewards a Christian eventually receives from the Holy One. A towering mountain of glittering rewards would never be meritorious enough to rescue a guilty sinner from the lake of fire.

Seeing Clearly for the First Time

It seems apparent that the Holy One intends to use the final judgment to drive home God's perspective on Christ's sacrifice. This heavenly moment of moral unmasking, *for the very first time*, will open the eyes of all humanity to the profound significance of Christ's sacrifice and the Father's gift of grace. For the first time, we will see, feel, and own the full weight, ugliness, destructive power, and wretched blasphemy of the parasitic, destructive thing called sin. For the first time, we will thoroughly understand how horribly deserving we are of God's condemnation and unending punishment for our sinfulness. We will finally see how deeply offensive, even repulsive, our wickedness has always been to the Holy One enthroned in heaven.

Hidden Holiness

We will finally understand the magnitude of God's unending grace and mercy as he patiently withheld his judgment throughout a frequently rebellious lifetime that so richly deserved his daily condemnation. We will finally begin to fully appreciate the magnitude of God's grace, love, care, and patience.

We will finally know something of the full measure of guilt, shame, and condemnation that Christ took onto his own shoulders as he hung from the cross at Calvary. We will begin to see the horror that must have erupted within Jesus' own being as the perfect, sinless Son of God not only experienced the penalty of his Father's judgment on human sin but also appropriated the guilt and shame of wicked, human rebellion as his very own, causing the Father to turn his back on his one and only Son.

We will finally understand how and why the crucified, resurrected Jesus is the only mediator between myself and the Father, and how absolutely naïve, ignorant, rebellious, and repugnant is every alternative proposal for a supposedly meaningful religious experience.

We will finally grasp the incomparable sacrifice made by the Holy One when he devised this plan to execute his perfect, eternal Son in order to expiate, to propitiate, the raging, rebellious blasphemies emanating from the noxious disobedience of every sinner who has ever lived.

The long-suffering patience, care, concern, mercy, devotion, commitment, fidelity, love, and grace of the Holy One will finally become apparent to all, blinding the legions of fallen humanity with the brilliance of God's true glory. Every human being will finally give this holy, savior God the full measure of praise, worship, and adoration that he has always deserved but never received until now. Even condemned unbelievers will glorify God for his righteousness and the fairness of his judgments.

Finally, we are now in a position to appreciate the most important objective of the Holy One's plan for salvation. For the grace of God works to recruit us into the army of saved sinners who will spend eternity exalting the glory of their holy, savior God. The fact that disciples receive the forgiveness of their sins and the promise

Holiness, History, and the End of It All

of eternal life is only gravy, folks—pure, gracious gravy dripping over the edges of God's spacious banqueting table. But the main meal is God's exaltation. We are not the centerpiece of God's story. God is. And all of God's works eventually point back to the Father as they find their fulfillment in him when they glorify his holiness.

Only on judgment day will these pressing, existential concerns be made crystal clear. And only then will we all sing with full-throated adoration that it is only right and true and just that the ultimate goal of our salvation has never been the forgiveness of our sins, but has always been the magnification of the glory, honor, and praise of the eternal Holy One, Father, Son and Holy Spirit.

In that auspicious moment of truth, we will praise God for issuing his judgment over our fallen lives because it was only through his revelation of final judgment that the scales fell from our eyes, allowing us to see the truth of who we truly are in the presence of the Holy One. Only then will we be fully equipped to join enthusiastically with the angels in singing:

> Holy, holy, holy is the Lord God Almighty, who was, and is, and is to come.
> You are worthy, our Lord and God to receive glory and honor and power;
> for you created all things, and by your will they were created and have their being.
> Worthy is the Lamb who was slain to receive power and wealth
> and wisdom and strength and honor and glory and praise!
> To him who sits on the throne and to the Lamb be praise and honor
> and glory and power for ever and ever! Amen

Discussion Questions:

1. Explain the concept of retributive justice and the relationship between God's holiness and God's wrath.

2. Many people do not like to think of God as a wrathful God. Yet, why is this dimension of God's person vital to a proper understanding of God's holiness?

3. In how many different ways does a biblical understanding of the final judgment lead us to give God praise, worship, and adoration?

4. As you meditate on the future, panoramic display of God's wrath and final redemption, spend time now worshiping the Holy One for who he is and what he has accomplished for you.

Bibliography

Abbott, Edwin A. *Flatland: A Romance of Many Dimensions*. London: Seeley, 1884; Garden City, NY: Dover, 1952.
Almond, Philip C. *Rudolf Otto: An Introduction to His Philosophical Theology*. Chapel Hill: University of North Carolina, 1984.
Aristophanes. *Four Plays: Clouds, Birds, Lysistrata, Women of the Assembly*. Translated by Aaron Poochigian. New York: Liveright, 2021.
Baird, J. A. *The Justice of God in the Teaching of Jesus*. London: SCM, 1963.
Barth, Karl. *The Christian Life*. Translated by G. F. Bromiley. Grand Rapids: Eerdmans, 1981.
———. *Church Dogmatics*. 2/1 *The Doctrine of God*. Translated by T. H. L. Parker et al. Edinburgh: T. & T. Clark, 1957.
———. *Church Dogmatics*. 4/4: *The Christian Life*. Translated by Geoffrey W. Bromiley. Grand Rapids: Eerdmans, 1981.
Bell, Daniel M. *The Economy of Desire: Christianity and Capitalism in a Postmodern World*. Grand Rapids: Baker Academic, 2012.
Boyd, Gregory. *Cross Vision: How the Crucifixion of Jesus Makes Sense of Old Testament Violence*. Minneapolis: Fortress, 2017.
Brünner, Emil. *The Christian Doctrine of God*. Translated by Olive Wyon. Philadelphia: Westminster, 1949.
Copan, P., and M. Flannagan. *Did God Really Command Genocide? Coming to Terms with the Justice of God*. Grand Rapids: Baker, 2014.
Crowder, C. "Rudolf Otto's *The Idea of the Holy* Revisited." In *Holiness Past & Present*, edited by Stephen C. Barton, 22–47. London: T. & T. Clark, 2003.
Crump, David. *I Pledge Allegiance: A Believer's Guide to Kingdom Citizenship in 21st Century America*. Grand Rapids: Eerdmans, 2018.
———. *Knocking on Heaven's Door: A New Testament Theology of Petitionary Prayer*. Grand Rapids: Baker Academic, 2006.
———. *Like Birds in a Cage: Christian Zionism's Collusion in Israel's Oppression of the Palestinian People*. Eugene, OR: Cascade, 2022.
Earl, D. S. *The Joshua Delusion? Rethinking Genocide in the Bible*. Eugene, OR: Cascade, 2010.
Gammie, John G. *Holiness in Israel*. Philadelphia: Augsburg Fortress, 1989.

Gundry, S. N., ed. *Four Views on God and Canaanite Genocide: Show Them No Mercy*. Grand Rapids: Zondervan, 2003.

Harrington, H. K. *Holiness: Rabbinic Judaism and the Graeco-Roman World*. London: Routledge, 2001.

Hodgson, R., Jr. "Holiness (NT)." In *The Anchor Bible Dictionary*, vol. 3, edited by David Noel Freedman et al., 249–54. New York: Doubleday, 1992.

Jenkins, Philip. *The Great and Holy War: How World War I Became a Religious Crusade*. New York: HarperCollins, 2014.

Keller, Timothy. *Generous Justice: How God's Grace Makes Us Just*. New York: Penguin, 2010.

Kierkegaard, Søren. *Philosophical Fragments*. Translated by Howard B. and Edna H. Hong. Princeton, NJ: Princeton University Press, 1985.

———. *Practice in Christianity*. Translated by Howard B. and Edna H. Hong. Princeton: Princeton University Press, 1991.

Lane, T. "The Wrath of God as an Aspect of God's Love." In *Nothing Greater, Nothing Better: Theological Essays on the Love of God*, edited by Kevin J. Vanhoozer, 138–67. Grand Rapids: Eerdmans, 2001.

Lind, Millard C. *Yahweh Is a Warrior: The Theology of Warfare in Ancient Israel*. Scottdale, PA: Herald, 1980.

Lüdemann, Gerd. *The Unholy in Holy Scripture: The Dark Side of the Bible*. Translated by John Bowden. Louisville: Westminster John Knox, 1997.

Morris, Leon. *The Apostolic Preaching of the Cross*. 3rd ed. Grand Rapids: Eerdmans, 1965.

———. *The Cross in the New Testament*. Grand Rapids: Eerdmans, 1965.

Otto, Rudolf. *The Idea of the Holy: An Inquiry into the Non-Rational Factor in the Idea of the Divine and Its Relation to the Rational*. Translated by John W. Harvey. Oxford: Oxford University Press, 1923.

Peterson, David. *Possessed by God: A New Testament Theology of Sanctification and Holiness*. Downers Grove, IL: InterVarsity, 1995.

Rothstein, Richard. *The Color of Law: A Forgotten History of How Our Government Segregated America*. New York: Liveright, 2017.

Shortt, Rupert. *Christianophobia: A Faith Under Attack*. Grand Rapids: Eerdmans, 2013.

Stern, Philip D. *The Biblical Herem: A Window on Israel's Religious Experience*. Atlanta: Scholars, 1991.

Strachan, Owen. *Christianity and Wokeness: How the Social Justice Movement is Hijacking the Gospel—and the Way to Stop It*. Washington, DC: Salem, 2021.

Tinker, M. *Mass Destruction: Is God Guilty of Genocide?* Garden City, UK: EP, 2017.

Trimm, Charlie. *The Destruction of the Canaanites: God, Genocide, and Biblical Interpretation*. Grand Rapids: Eerdmans, 2022.

Von Rad, Gerhard. *Old Testament Theology*. 2 volumes. Translated by D. M. G. Stalker. New York: Harper & Row, 1962.

Webster, John. *Holiness*. Grand Rapids: Eerdmans, 2003.

Bibliography

Wright, D. P. "Holiness (OT)." In *The Anchor Bible Dictionary*, vol. 3, edited by David Noel Freedman et al., 237–49 New York: Doubleday, 1992.

Scripture Index

Old Testament

Genesis

1:27	17

Exodus

3	28
3:5–6	3, 30
3:6	28
3:6–8	29
3:7–10	95
3:8	40
3:12	2 n2, 50
3:13–15	2
3:14–15	2 n2
3:17	40
13:5	40
19:4–6	50
19:5	50
19:5–6	53, 65
19:6	52
19:10–13	30
19:12	31 n16
19:18	21
19:22	3, 21, 31 n16, 46
19:22–24	30
19:24	3, 21, 31 n16, 46
20:6	80
23:10–12	86
23:11–12	89 n13
31:13	51
33:19	4
33:20	4, 21
33:23	4
34:6–8	4

Leviticus

6	51
6:18	51
6:27	51
10:1–2	31
10:3	31
11:44	64
11:44–45	xviii, 63, 66 n3
19	82
19:1	82
19:2	63 n1, 66 n3
19:9–10	86
19:18	67, 80
20:7	64, 66 n3
20:7–8	63
20:8	51
20:26	63 n1
21:8	63 n1
22:31–33	63 n1
25:1–17	86
25:8–17	87

Numbers

16:3	51, 52

Numbers (continued)

16:31–33	53
16:35–39	53

Deuteronomy

5:10	80
6:5	80
7:1–2	40
7:6	51
14:2	51
14:21	51
15:4	86, 88
15:8	86
15:11	86
20:16–17	40
23:24–25	87
24:17	83
24:19–22	87
26:19	51
28:1–14	46
28:9	51
28:15–68	5, 46
32:35	94

Joshua

6	32
6:15	32
6:17–27	32
6:21	40
6:24	40
6:25–26	32
7:15–26	40

1 Samuel

6:20	22

2 Samuel

6:6–7	32
7:22	19

Job

36:26	17, 21

Psalms

68:4–6	82
72:12–14	82
72:19	29
97:1–6	57
99:2–4	78
99:4	82
140:12	82

Proverbs

1:7	25
26:11	59
29:7	82

Isaiah

1:16–17	83
3:13–15	85
4:3	51
5:16	83
6:1–8	28–29
8:22	44 n11
10:1–2	85
10:2	86
11:4	83
37:16	19
41:14	30 n15
42:1	83
43:3	30 n15
47:4	30 n15
48:17	30 n15
49:7	30 n15
51:5	83
54:5	30 n15
55:5	19
55:8–9	15
57:15	19
58:6–10	85
61:8	83

Scripture Index

Jeremiah

13:11	51
15:9	44 n11
22:1–5	85
31:31–34	9

Ezekiel

13:19	6 n4
20:9	6 n4
20:14	6 n4
20:22	6 n4
22:26	6 n4
22:29	83
26:23	31
34:1–10	9 n6
34:17–22	9 n6
34:23–24	9
35:1–14	9 n6
36:1–7	9 n6
36:16–20	9 n6
36:20–23	6
36:21	7
36:22–23	6
36:24–28	9
37:22–25	9
38:16	7
38:22–23	9
38:23	7
39:7	6 n4, 7
39:21	7
39:25	7
39:27	7
44:19	52

Daniel

9:4	80

Joel

2:2	44 n11
2:10	44 n11
2:30–31	44 n11
3:1–5	44 n11
3:15	44 n11

Amos

4:2	19
5:11–12	85
5:24	77, 79
6:8	19
8:9	44 n11

Habakkuk

3:3	19

Zephaniah

1:15	44 n11

Malachi

3:5	83

New Testament

Matthew

1:23	4
5:6	79
5:9	47
5:10	79
5:44–48	47
5:45	96
6:9–34	2
7:13–14	32
7:23	33
10:11–20	98
10:40–42	98
12:18–20	83
12:48–50	98
18:2–6	98
22:37–40	65
25:31–46	97–98
25:34	98
25:40	97
25:41	98
25:45	97

Scripture Index

Matthew (continued)

27:45	44

Mark

2:23–24	87
12:30–31	80
13:26–27	92
15:33	44

Luke

1:6	79
3:8–9	33
3:10–14	83
11:2–4	2
11:42	83
15:11–32	69
17:20–37	70
17:33	70
22:41–44	73
23:44–45	44

John

1:18	22
10:28–29	10
14:6	32
14:15	80
15:18	94

Acts

2:17–21	44 n11
2:23	44
2:44–45	88
3:18	44
4:28	44
4:32–35	88
5:1–11	33
5:6	33
5:10	33
9:13	53–54 n1, 65 n2
9:32	53–54 n1, 65 n2
9:41	53–54 n1, 65 n2
10:34	83

Romans

1:7	53 n1, 65 n2
1:18–20	27
2:11	83
6:17–23	68
7:15–20	68
8:3	44
8:17	70, 71
8:18–27	72
8:27	53 n1, 65 n2
9	36, 39
9:1–21	36
9:6–9	36
9:10–13	37
9:11–12	37
9:13b	37
9:14–15	37
9:18	37
9:19–21	38
9:22–23	38
11:33–36	39
11:34	48
12:1–29	66–67 n4
12:13	53 n1, 65 n2
12:13–17	60
12:19	94
15:16	54
15:25–27	53 n1, 65 n2
15:31	53 n1, 65 n2
16:2	53 n1, 65 n2

1 Corinthians

1:2	53 n1, 54, 65 n2
3:13–15	100
6:1–2	53 n1, 65 n2
6:11	54
7:14	55
11:27–30	34
13:12	15
14:33	53 n1, 65 n2
15:43	101

Scripture Index

16:1	53–54 n1, 65 n2
16:15	53–54 n1, 65 n2

2 Corinthians

1:1	53–54 n1, 65 n2
3:2–18	66–67 n4
3:18	101
4:17	101
4:17–18	75
5:10	100
8:4	53–54 n1, 65 n2
9:1	53–54 n1, 65 n2
9:12	53–54 n1, 65 n2
13:12	53–54 n1, 65 n2

Galatians

5:13–14	67
5:13–26	66–68
5:14	80
5:16–17	65
5:16–19	67
5:19–21	66, 68
5:21	69
5:22–23	95
5:22–26	69
5:24	67, 68, 69
5:25	67
6:2	60

Ephesians

1:1	53–54 n1, 65 n2
4:12	53–54 n1, 65 n2
4:22–5:21	66–67 n4
5:6	94
5:26	54
6:9	83

Philippians

1:1	53–54 n1, 65 n2

Colossians

1:2	53–54 n1, 65 n2
3:1–17	66–67 n4
3:6	94
3:25	83

1 Thessalonians

2:16	94, 95
4:1–10	66–67 n4
5:1–11	94

2 Thessalonians

1:5–10	96
1:10	71, 101
2:14	101

1 Timothy

1:17	19
6:15–16	22

2 Timothy

2:14–26	66–67 n4
3:12	94

Titus

1:7–16	66–67 n4

Hebrews

2:10	70
2:17	72
2:18	70, 72
4:15	44, 72
8:7–33	9 n5
10:30–31	22
12:2	67
12:14	66, 69
12:28	22

Scripture Index

James

1:27	81
2:1	83
2:1–7	88
2:8	80
2:9	83
2:12–13	90
4:1–12	66–67 n4

1 Peter

1:2	53
1:13–2:3	66–67 n4
1:15–16	65–66
1:16	xviii
2:9	53, 65
2:22	44
4:1	74
4:1–19	66–67 n4
4:16b-17	71
4:17	100
5:4	101
5:10	75, 101

2 Peter

3:11	66

Revelation

4:10	5
6:10	95
14:19	95
15:1	99
15:3–4	99
16:5–7	99
18	95
19:2a	95
19:2d	95
19:15c	95
20:11–15	100
20:12c	100
20:13c	100
20:15	100
22:12	100

Subject Index

Aaron, 31, 52
abandonment, 82
Abbott, Edwin A., 13
Abihu, 31
Achan, 32, 40
acquisition/greed, 74
adoration/worship of God
   at final judgment, 95, 98–99, 102–3
   his people and, 59, 93
   holy war as, 40
   inadequacy of, 8
   by Moses, 4
agency/freedom of humans, 10, 27 n9
agriculture, 86–87
aliens/foreigners (non-Israelites), 83
al-Qaida, xvi
altar of tabernacle, 52
America, xv, xvi, 74, 77, 78 n5, 84–85, 84 n8, 88
Ananias, 33
animals, care of, 87, 89 n13
apostles, 1, 88. *See also* disciples of Jesus Christ
ark of the covenant, 22, 32
arrogance/pride, xvi, 74
Assyrian exile, 89
authenticity/transparency, 60–62

Babylon, whore of (Revelation), 95
Babylonian captivity, 5–7, 30, 89
Ball, Mr., 14–15, 18, 20
Barth, Karl, 16, 21–22, 56
Beth Shemesh, 21–22
the Bible/Scriptures, xix, 2–4, 41, 56–57, 79, 92. *See also* revelation of God
The Biblical Herem: A Window on Israel's Religious Experience (Stern), 43
blasphemy, xv–xvii, xv n1, 64, 101–2
blessings
   of the covenant, 6–8, 46
   of revelation, 22
   of salvation through Jesus Christ, 94, 99
   on those who long for justice, 79
body of Christ (believers), 53–55
book of life, 100–101
Boyd, Gregory, 41, 41 n7, 44
brokenness, 62, 71, 78–79 n6
Brünner, Emil, 26 n6, 27 n9, 30
burning bush, 3, 28

Calvin University, xvii
Canaan/Canaanites, 39–41, 40–41 n6, 43, 44 n11, 45–47. *See also* war, holy

Subject Index

captivity/exile, 5–7, 30, 89
charity/generosity, 85–89, 97
choice/election of people, 36–37, 53, 92
Christ, body of (believers), 53–55
Christianity and Wokeness: How the Social Justice Movement is Hijacking the Gospel-and the Way to Stop It (Strachan), 77, 77 n4, 87 n11
the church
  continuity with Israel, 53–55, 65, 85
  heresy in, 41, 63–64
  Jesus Christ and, 53–55, 66
  judgment in, 33–34
  justice and, 88–89
  participation in, 59–60
  redemption and, 64, 85
  social justice and, 77, 84–85, 90
  suffering in, 71, 94–95, 98
  as welcoming and authentic, 60
communion/Lord's Supper, 33–34
condemnation
  by God, 3, 9, 83, 86, 90, 94–95, 98–102
  of heresy, 64
  by others, 43, 94
confession of sin, 58–60
consecration, 2, 21, 40, 40 n4, 51–52, 63–65. *See also* sanctification
Corinth, 33–34
the cosmos. *See* the world/cosmos
covenant, new
  approaching God in, 32–34
  continuity with Sinaitic covenant, 53–55, 65–66
  differences from Sinaitic covenant, 46–47, 65
  election in, 53, 92
  establishment of, 5, 10, 46, 65
  in Ezekiel, 8–9
  fulfillment of, 10–11
  in Jeremiah, 9, 9 n5

covenant, Sinaitic/old
  approaching God in, 3, 30–31, 46, 52–53
  breaking of, 5–6, 30–32, 44 n11, 46
  election in, 36–37
  establishment of, 3, 46, 50
  promises in, 6–8, 46
  requirements of, 64–65, 80
  sacrifices in, 31, 51–52
creation, new, 88
critical race theory, 77
crops, agricultural, 86–87
crucifixion of Jesus Christ, 43–45, 57, 65, 68, 81, 102
crying, 61–62
curse words, xv, 2
curses, 46–47, 98

darkness at crucifixion, 44
David, 32
the Day of the Lord, 44. *See also* judgment of God
death, 30–31, 33–34, 44–45, 53, 72. *See also* crucifixion of Jesus Christ
The Destruction of the Canaanites: God, Genocide, and Biblical Interpretation (Trimm), 45
difficulties/struggles, 57, 59–60, 71–73, 75. *See also* suffering
dikaiosunē, 79. *See also* justice; righteousness
disciples of Jesus Christ, 1–2, 10, 31, 72, 94, 97–98. *See also* apostles
discrimination/racism, 79, 81, 83–84, 84 n8
discussion questions, 11, 22–23, 35, 48, 62, 75–76, 90, 103–4
disease/sickness, 1, 34, 72
disobedience/rebellion. *See also* sin
  of believers, 57–58, 68–69
  hostility against God and, 94

Subject Index

of Israel, 5–6, 6 n4, 30–32, 44 n11, 46, 83, 89–90
punishment for, 9, 30, 44, 44 n11, 94–95, 99, 102
sinful nature and, 67–69
suffering and, 75
divorce, 55
Downs, George W., xvii

eclipses, 44
Egyptian bondage, 27, 29, 50, 81
election/choice of people, 36–37, 53, 92
Elizabeth, 79
Emmanuel, 4
empathy, 59–60
enemies
of believers, 46–47, 94
of God, 44–45, 44 n11
of Israel, xvi
environmentalism, 89, 89 n13
equity, 77, 78 n5, 80, 82–89
Esau, 37
eternal life, 34, 70, 103
ethics, 12, 26, 43, 51, 64, 69–70, 85. *See also* morality
evangelicals, American, 77, 78 n5, 84
exile/captivity, 5–7, 30, 89
Ezekiel, 5–10, 6 n4

failure. *See* sin
faith in Jesus Christ, 29, 47–48, 54–55, 66–67
faithfulness
of believers, 68–69, 72, 74, 94
of God, 2 n2, 6–7, 10, 46
farming, 86–87
favoritism, 83, 88
fear of God, 3–4, 22, 25, 28, 33, 52
feelings, 60 n8, 68 n5
Flatland: A Romance of Many Dimensions (Abbott), 13–15, 18, 20

foreigners/aliens (non-Israelites), 83
forgiveness of sins, 9, 22, 56, 102–3
freedom/agency of humans, 10, 27 n9
fruit of the Holy Spirit, 69, 72, 93

Gaza Strip, 61
generosity/charity, 85–89, 97
genocide, 40, 47
glory
of Christians/believers, 70, 75
of God, 3–5, 8, 10, 38, 70–71, 98–103
of Jesus Christ, 70, 92, 96
God. *See also* the Holy Spirit; Jesus Christ; name of God
approaching, 3–4, 21–22, 27–28, 30–34, 46, 52–53
attributes/character of, 7–8, 12, 19–20, 28, 83, 102
false view of, 17, 19, 34
grace of, 4, 15 n3, 49–50, 56, 93, 102
honoring, 2, 8, 56, 103
image of, 17, 27, 78–79, 78–79 n6, 83–84
love of, 19, 33–35, 44, 49–50, 57–58, 81, 94
mercy of, 37–38, 90, 102
mystery/hiddenness of, 21–22, 25, 28, 29, 47–49
presence of, 3, 50–53, 55, 96
as qualitatively different, 7, 15–22, 15 n3, 19 n6, 26–27, 27 n9, 30–31, 56
Gog, 7, 9
grace of God, 4, 15 n3, 49–50, 56, 93, 102
The Great and Holy War: How World War I Became a Religious Crusade (Jenkins), xvi
greed/acquisition, 74
Greeks, ancient, xv, xv n1

Subject Index

ground, holy, xvi, 3, 30–31
guidance of the Holy Spirit, 59, 67–69, 68 n5
guilt, 57–59, 84, 93, 102

hallowed, 2, 8
ḥērem, 40–41, 40 n3–4, 43, 45. *See also* war, holy
heresy, 41, 41 n7, 63–64
hiddenness of God, 21–22, 25, 28–29, 47–49
history, human, 6–7, 10, 38, 85, 92
holiness of God. *See also* hiddenness of God; war, holy
  meaning of, 8, 12–13, 19–20, 19 n6, 26–29
  as contagious, 3, 51–52, 55
  disrespecting, xv–xvii, 32–34
  justice and, 77–78, 81, 83
  love and, 34–35
holiness of God's people
  as gift, 50–51, 53–55, 58, 63, 65, 67
  as responsibility, 12, 50, 63–69, 70, 93
  justice and, 79–83
  suffering and, 69–75
holy ground, xvi, 3, 30–31
the Holy Spirit
  fruit of, 69, 72, 93
  gift of, 8–10, 93
  grieving, 57, 69
  guidance of, 59, 67–69, 68 n5
  holiness and, 58, 67, 70, 93
  indwelling of, 55
  keeping in step with, 66–68, 71, 74–75
  lying to, 33
  suffering and, 71
holy war. *See* war, holy
honesty, 60
honoring God, 2, 8, 56, 103
humanity/humans
  agency/freedom of, 10, 27 n9

  as different from God, 7, 15–22, 15 n3, 19 n6, 26–27, 27 n9, 30–31, 56
  final judgment of, 100–101
  image of God in, 17, 27, 78–79, 78–79 n6, 83–84
  sinful nature of, 66–69, 72
  understanding God, 4, 8, 17, 25
humility, 7, 22

I Pledge Allegiance: A Believer's Guide to Kingdom Citizenship in 21st-Century America (Crump), 69–70
The Idea of the Holy (Otto), 24–26
image of God *(imago Dei)*, 17, 27, 78–79, 78–79 n6, 83, 84
immigrants, 85
incarnation of Jesus Christ, 4, 15 n3, 22
incense, 31, 52
individualism, 84–85, 88
inequity. *See* equity
injustice. *See* justice; oppression
Isaac, 36–37
Isaiah, 28–29
Ishmael, 36
Israel, ancient. *See also* covenant, Sinaitic/old; war, holy
  Assyrian exile and, 89
  Babylonian captivity and, 5–7, 30, 89
  disobedience of, 5–6, 6 n4, 30, 32, 44 n11, 46, 83, 89–90
  Egyptian bondage and, 27, 29, 50, 81
  priests of, 31, 51–53, 64
  promised land and, 6, 43, 46
  rescue of, 6–7, 29–30, 50, 99
  social welfare in, 85–88
Israel, modern, 61–62

Jacob, 37
Jenkins, Philip, xvi
Jericho, 32, 40

Subject Index

Jesus Christ. *See also* covenant, new
  the church and, 53–55, 66
  crucifixion of, 43–45, 57, 65, 68, 81, 102
  ethical instructions of, 69–70
  faith in, 29, 47–48, 54–55, 66–67
  incarnation of, 4, 15 n3, 22
  judgment and, 33, 95
  return of, 66, 92, 101
  as revelation of God, 41, 43–44
  salvation through, 66, 70, 81, 94
  suffering of, 10, 46, 70–74
  teaching on prayer of, 2–3, 5–6, 10–11
Jews, 1–3, 36, 65, 100 n1
John the Baptist, 79, 83
Joshua, 40, 40 n1, 45–47
Jubilee, Year of, 87
judgment of God. *See also* Babylonian captivity
  at crucifixion, 44–45, 102
  in early church, 33–34
  final, 33, 44, 46, 66, 71, 93–103
  his people and, 22, 66, 71, 90, 95, 97–98, 100
  withholding of, 102
Julian (Roman emperor), 89
justice. *See also* judgment of God
  definition of, 78–80
  equity and, 78 n5, 87
  holiness of God and, 77–78, 81, 83
  responsibility of God's people for, 79–83
  retributive, 89–90, 93–97
  social, 84–89

Kierkegaard, Søren, 16–17, 48
kingdom of God
  description of, 22, 98
  admittance to, 32, 59, 66, 69, 79
  values of, 69–70, 79
Korah, 52–53

land, promised, 6, 43, 46. *See also* Canaan/Canaanites
law, modern, 84–85, 89
law of God, 64–65, 67, 79–80, 82–83, 85–87
Levites, 52, 64
life
  book of, 100–101
  eternal, 34, 70, 103
  losing one's, 70
the Lord's Prayer, 2, 10, 31, 99
the Lord's Supper/communion, 33–34
love
  for enemies, 47
  for God, 65, 74, 80–81, 93
  God's, 19, 33–35, 44, 49–50, 57–58, 81, 94
  for others, 60, 64–67, 80–82, 93–94
Lüdemann, Gerd, 41–44

Marcion, 41, 41 n7
marriage, 55
martyrdom, 72, 94
mercy of God, 37–38, 90, 102
morality, 12, 26, 43, 58, 67–68, 81. *See also* ethics
Moses, 3–5, 21, 28–31, 40 n1, 52–53
Mother Theresa of Calcutta, 97
mystery/hiddenness of God, 21–22, 25, 28–29, 47–49

Nadab, 31
name of God
  meaning of, 2, 2 n2
  abuse of, xv
  hallowing/glorifying, 2–3, 7–10, 99
  Jewish use of, 2–3
  profaning, 6, 6 n4
nation, chosen/holy, 46, 50, 53–54, 65
nature, sinful, 66–69, 72

Subject Index

new covenant. *See* covenant, new
new creation, 88

obedience. *See also* disobedience/rebellion
   Christians/believers and, 54, 66, 68–70, 80
   freedom and, 27 n9
   relationship with God and, 29
   Sinaitic covenant and, 30, 46, 50, 64
obligation/responsibility, 27 n9, 63, 65–66, 69, 85–86
old covenant. *See* covenant, Sinaitic/old
Old Testament, 41–48, 41 n7, 44 n11, 85, 89 n13
oppression, 8, 81–83, 93, 98. *See also* suffering
Otto, Louis Karl Rudolf, 24–26, 26 n6, 28, 35

Packer, J. I., xix
Palestine, 61–62
Patch, Harry, xvi
persecution of Christians/believers, 71, 94–95, 98
perseverance, 72, 75
Peterson, David, 54–55
Pharisees, 83
Possessed by God: A New Testament Theology of Sanctification and Holiness (Peterson), 54
poverty, 81–83, 85–88, 90, 97–98
praise. *See* adoration/worship of God
prayer, 2–3, 5–6, 10, 57
pride/arrogance, xvi, 74
priests, Israelite, 31, 51–53, 64
promised land, 6, 43, 46. *See also* Canaan/Canaanites
property, personal, 85–87
punishment
   for covenant breaking, 5–6, 30–32, 44 n11, 46
   final judgment and, 46, 95–96, 99
   God's name and, 9, 99
   Jesus Christ taking ours, 44, 102
   retributive, 89–90, 93–94
purification, 64–65, 71

qadosh, 26, 40

race theory, critical, 77
racism/discrimination, 79, 81, 83–84, 84 n8
Rad, Gerhard von, 19 n6
rebellion. *See* disobedience/rebellion
Red Sea, 50
redemption. *See also* salvation
   the church and, 64, 85
   God as redeemer, 30, 32–35, 64, 93–94, 99
   holy war and, 43
   in marriage, 55
   obedience and, 30, 101
relationships
   with God, 2, 26–31, 46, 49–50, 58, 93
   with others, 59–62, 64, 67, 79–80, 83, 88
repentance, 33, 58–59, 69, 84, 89
rescue. *See* salvation
responsibility/obligation, 27 n9, 63, 65–66, 69, 85–86
retribution, 89–90, 93–97
return of Jesus Christ, 66, 92, 101
revelation of God. *See also* the Scriptures/Bible
   final judgment and, 103
   Jesus Christ as, 41, 43–44
   knowing God through, 16–17, 27, 29, 31, 92–93
   not exhaustive, 20–22
revenge/vengeance, 47, 93–95

Subject Index

righteousness
  definition of, 12–13, 79–81
  of Christians/believers, 68–69
  at final judgment, 71
  of God, 83, 102
  justice and, 79–83
  lack of, 101

sacrifice
  of Christians/believers, 70–71, 82
  during holy war, 40
  of Jesus Christ, 44–45, 65, 81, 102
  in Sinaitic covenant, 31, 51–52
salvation. *See also* redemption
  goal of, 99, 102–3
  God's name and, 8–10
  through Jesus Christ, 66, 70, 81, 94
sanctification. *See also* consecration
  meaning of, xvi–xvii, 12, 54
  of Christians/believers, 54–55, 58–59, 65, 67, 71
  of God's name, 3, 6, 6 n4, 8–10
  of the Lord's Supper, 33–34
  through God, 52–53
  of unbelievers, 55
Sapphira, 33
Satan, 44
the Scriptures/Bible, xix, 2–4, 41, 56–57, 79, 92. *See also* revelation of God
the Second Coming. *See* return of Jesus Christ
self-awareness, 74
self-control, 74
self-denial, 70
self-promotion, 74
separation
  between God and humans, 15–22, 26–27
  from God at final judgment, 96, 98

holiness and, 12–13, 26, 64
servanthood, 74, 82
sex, illicit, 13, 68, 74
shame, 57–58, 102
sheep and goats, 97–98
sickness/disease, 1, 34, 72
signs, heavenly, 44
sin. *See also* judgment of God; repentance
  confession of, 58–60
  forgiveness of, 9, 22, 56, 102–3
  holiness of God and, 4, 12
  persistent, 69
  sacrifice for, 44–45
  sinful nature and, 66–69, 72
  slavery to, 93
  societal, 84
  suffering and, 73–75
Sinai, Mount, 3–4, 21, 31, 46, 50, 53, 80
Sinaitic/old covenant. *See* covenant, Sinaitic/old
sinful nature, 66–69, 72
slavery
  Babylonian, 5–7, 30, 89
  Egyptian, 27, 29, 50, 81
  to righteousness, 68
  to sin, 93
sovereignty of God, 36–39, 43, 52–53
Spaceland, 13–15
Spirit, Holy. *See* the Holy Spirit
Stern, Philip D., 43
Strachan, Owen, 77, 77 n4, 87 n11
struggles/difficulties, 57, 59–60, 71–73, 75. *See also* suffering
substitutionary death, 44
suffering
  role of, 69–75
  types of, 74–75
  of Christians/believers, 69–75, 94–96, 98
  of Israelites, 29
  of Jesus Christ, 10, 46, 70–74
  of others, 81–83

Subject Index

swear words, xv, 2
synagogue, Moroccan, 25–26

tabernacle, 31–32, 51–52
temptations, 57, 68, 70, 72–74
terror, war against, xvi
theology, xix, 16, 26, 46
Theresa, Mother, of Calcutta, 97
transformation of Christians/
    believers, 59, 70, 84
transparency/authenticity, 60–62
treasure, holy, 50–51, 53, 55,
    59–60
Trimm, Charlie, 45–46
Twin Towers (New York City), xvi

*The Unholy in Holy Scripture: The
    Dark Side of the Bible* (Lüde-
    mann), 42–43
the United States of America, xv,
    xvi, 74, 77, 84, 84 n8
Uzzah, 32

vengeance/revenge, 47, 93–95
violence, divine, 36–48. *See also*
    war, holy
von Rad, Gerhard, 19 n6

war, holy
    definition of, xvi
    reason for, 43, 44 n11
    conquest of Canaan as, 39–41,
        40–41 nn3–4 and 6, 43

heavenly signs and, 44
Jesus Christ's crucifixion as,
    44–45
misuse of, 45–46
offensiveness of, 47–48
World War I as, xvi–xvii
wealth, 86–88
Webster, John, 19–20
welfare system, 85–87, 89 n13, 90
the West Bank, 61
the wicked, 71, 99
winepress of fury, 95
wokeness, 77, 84
World War I, xvi–xvii
the world/cosmos. *See also* war,
    holy
    Christians/believers in, 64, 68,
        71–72, 94, 97–98
    fallen, 12, 15, 19 n6, 64, 71–72
    God distinct from, 26
    God glorified in, 10, 29
    God rescues, 35
    God's revelation to, 27
    judgment of, 95, 98
worship. *See* adoration/worship
    of God
wrath of God, 33, 41, 44–45, 55,
    94–95, 98–99

Yahweh, 2–3, 2 n2. *See also* God
Year of Jubilee, 87

Zechariah, 79

www.ingramcontent.com/pod-product-compliance
Lightning Source LLC
Chambersburg PA
CBHW020854160426
43192CB00007B/917